GET RICH

WITH

Y2K

HOW TO CASH IN ON THE FINANCIAL
CRISIS IN THE YEAR 2000

By
STEVEN L. PORTER

PICCADILLY BOOKS
COLORADO SPRINGS, CO

Piccadilly Books
P.O. Box 25203
Colorado Springs, CO 80936

Distributed by
  Empire Publishing Service
  P.O. Box 1344
  Studio City, CA 91614, USA

Library of Congress Cataloging-in-Publication Data
Porter, Steven L., 1952-
        Get rich with Y2K: how to cash in on the financial crisis in the year 2000/ Steven L. Porter.
        p. cm.
    Includes index.
    ISBN 0-941599-48-5
    1. Real estate investment--United States. 2. House buying--United States. 3. Real property--United States--Purchasing. 4. Foreclosure--United States. 5. Government sale of real property--United States. 6. Year 2000 date conversion (Computer systems)--United States. 7. Financial crises--United States. I. Title.
    HD255 .P67 1999
    332.63'24--dc21   98-54141

Printed in USA

TABLE OF CONTENTS

1

THE Y2K CRISIS

We are about to face possibly the most terrifying and challenging time of our lives. With the world economy on a downward spiral and the consequences of the year 2000 computer flaw, commonly known as Y2K, we could be facing the worst economic recession since the Great Depression. No one really knows how bad things are going to be, or if things will be any more serious than any of the numerous recessions we encounter just about every decade or so. What you can count on, are some rough times ahead for the next few years. This book was written to help you cope financially with the trouble that lies ahead and to show you how to turn it to your advantage. In fact, the opportunity for acquiring financial riches is mind boggling. And the opportunity is best whenever there is an economic downturn, the bigger, the better. Many shrewd investors have accumulated millions of dollars in profits during recessions by taking advantage of the economic climate, with this book as your guide, you can too.

BLACKOUT

In the summer of 1996 my family and I were driving up to Yellowstone National Park. As we passed through the town of Rexburg, Idaho all the traffic lights suddenly went dead. Cars coming from both ways shot across intersections, narrowly missing each other. We turned onto a side street to avoid the mayhem. Sirens soon blared in response to dozens of accidents that had occurred in a matter of minutes.

We walked past several stores, most were closed with their doors locked. Yet, many still had what appeared to be customers inside. After walking for awhile we found one grocery store with its doors open and customers busily streaming in and out as if hurriedly buying supplies to last them the winter. It was chaos inside. The lights were out. Nervous shoppers groped around in the dark, clerks with flashlights guided people as best they could. Automatic doors didn't work and clerks stood guard to prevent theft.

The whole town was without electricity. Everything was off. We got a motel room but the lights, TV, radio, and air conditioner didn't work. Too hot to just say couped up in a dark room. We went outside, but as nighttime approached, without lights of any type, the entire place looked dark and spooky. Most all businesses had closed down. People stayed home except to buy food. We went back to our motel room and stayed the night with nothing to do but sleep. I reflected how much our lives depend electricity.

What happened? We learned later that a tree limb fell on a power line cutting off the electricity to seven western states and parts of Canada and Mexico. This massive power outage shut down every business and government agency in western part of the continent as well as knocking out mass transportation and water pumps and many, many other utilities. That's scary.

This event was just a temporary power failure and power returned a few hours later. But what would have happened if electricity in the entire country went down and stayed down for days, weeks, or months? What if water and sewage lines stopped flowing? Telephone lines went down? What if computers that control the financial institutions, businesses, and governments of this country suddenly went berserk. What chaos that would bring. This could be what it's gong to be like on January 1, 2000.

Impossible you say?... It could happen. That's what the Y2K crisis is all about. Although no one knows how serious the problem will be, there *will* be problems and the economy *will* suffer.

Among computer users Y2K stands for the year 2000. At midnight on December 31, 1999 computer clocks may or may not work. This might not sound too threatening but it can cause any number of problems including the creation of erroneous data or complete computer breakdown. Since computers control almost everything in our lives, this means electricity, water, gas, everything we depend on may stop working on January 1, 2000. The result will be a severe economic crisis.

THE COMPUTER BUG

The Y2K problem began back in the early days of computers when it took a room-sized mainframe to do what a hand-held calculator can do today. Programmers saved precious and costly computer memory space by using a two-digit shorthand to represent years. Each year being represented by its last two digits rather than by all four—1972 became 72. Unpredictable consequences happen as computers roll over from 99 to 00. Does the computer recognize it as the year 2000 or 1900 or simply freeze up, not knowing what to do?

The immediate savings gained justified the practice and besides, there was plenty of time to adjust the system before the year 2000. Many believed these older systems would be replaced before that time. But new computer software is usually made compatible with older systems, perpetuating the two-digit representation. With the Y2K computer bug imbedded in the vast majority of computer systems, businesses, organizations, and governments are left to correct a coding decision made decades ago.

A few examples of what could go wrong if computes are not fixed in time:

- A telephone call that begins just before midnight Dec. 31, 1999, and ends minutes later on Jan, 1, 2000, could be billed as a 99-year conversation.

- Many ATM machines will refuse to spit out money.

- A credit card bill owed on Jan. 7, 2000, could be mistaken as 99 years past due.

- Social Security computers might refuse to issue a check to a woman born in 1912 because it might appear she hasn't been born yet.

- Computers that regulate the flow of electricity through power grids could become confused, producing widespread blackouts while similar problems could disrupt, telephone service and shut off water supplies.

- Some coffee makers won't brew.

- Even some of America's weapons system might not work.

Tests of computers that do all sorts of jobs show the problem is very real. For example, when Chrysler rolled its clocks forward to simulate 2000 at one of its Michigan assembly plants, computerized security gates wouldn't let anyone in or out.

The size of the job is staggering. In the United States alone, there are 157 billion software functions that need to be checked, according to Casper Jones of Software Productivity Research, a software consulting firm in Burlington, Mass.

The old mainframe computers still used by government and big corporations for many vital functions are particularly vulnerable. But the electronics industry has found that tiny computer chips known as microprocessors which are in everything from coffee makers to oil tankers are date sensitive and, therefore, susceptible to the Y2K problem. These microprocessors can not be reprogrammed and must physically be replaced. There are literally *millions* of these microprocessors currently in use in innumerable products in both industry and in our households.

SOLVING THE PROBLEM

Computers control everything from assembly lines at General Motors to nuclear power plants. Experts are predicting that costs from both correcting the problem and malfunction repercussions could drain business profits enough to cause a significant economic downturn. And as the new millennium approaches, it is becoming clearer that many companies, government agencies, and others will *not* be ready on time.

Surprisingly, many people are not concerned and continue to ask, "Why not just fix the numbers?"

This is a problem that on the surface appears relatively trivial and even simple to solve. But the use of dates in modern business systems is absolutely ubiquitous. The two-digit problem is analogous to a cancer that has metastasized throughout the body. Many computer experts believe the Y2K problem is bigger—possibly much bigger—than anticipated. Warnings have gone out to business and government leaders to act quickly and decisively against the Y2K problem.

Even a single neglected two-digit abbreviation could send bad data rippling outward, causing fallout ranging from the relatively innocuous to the catastrophic. Vulnerable are everything and everyone dependent on computers—government agencies, utilities, subways, trains. Even devices not generally thought of as computer dependent have "embedded" systems—tiny computer chips like those in elevators and cars. Many chips are date-sensitive and could malfunction when their date attempts to roll over to the year 2000.

A scenario could look like this: If a computer is checking expiration dates on a product in a factory and it interprets "00" as 1900, any product stamped "00" might be deemed out-of-date and diverted to a conveyer belt headed for a dumpster. Dry runs simulating the rollover to 2000 have resulted in hypothetical factory shutdowns, payroll delays, and deadly chemicals being dumped into drinking water.

Unless a system has been tested specifically for a double zero glitch, no one really knows what any particular software will tell the system to do. All kinds of weird things can end up happening.

The task is not particularly complex, but the volume of computer applications and code that must be inspected is gargantuan. Forty years worth of software has to be checked, fixed, tested, and revised in a period of time woefully too short.

Experts stated as far back as 1997 that, "Even if every company started working on the Y2K bug today, there is not enough time left or skilled workers available to take care of the problem. The manpower needed to correct the problem really goes beyond our resources."

The number of hours that will have to be spent is mind boggling. Companies running large mainframe computers with customized software are faced with analyzing literally *millions* of lines of computer code and making appropriate changes. Citibank alone has 400 million lines of software code to inspect and GM has two billion. Companies using hardware and software purchased "off the shelf" (preassembled computers or prepackaged software) need to test their systems for Y2K compliance, work with vendors to correct problems, and implement solutions. It is an overwhelming problem. It won't be finished by the year 2000. Some won't be finished even by 2001 or beyond. There's simply too much work to do and not enough time left to do it.

Complicating clean-up efforts is the fact that most computer business systems were written using COBOL, a computer language rarely used any more. Most universities don't even teach it and many computer engineers don't know COBOL, and thus cannot effectively de-bug programs for the Y2K problem.

This has opened up a whole new avenue for retired COBOL programmers. If you have these skills and are retired, there's a place for you.

Any particular company solving its own Y2K problems is just one layer of the problem. Companies continually interact—exchanging data and depending on one another for information—creating a cascading effect.

One company may be completely compliant with year 2000 processing, and yet, if we're getting electronic data from someone—say an outside supplier or a customer that sends orders or pays bills or whatever—and they're not compliant, we still have a problem if they are exchanging corrupt data. And they may even say they're compliant and think they are, but they're not. For that matter, we may think we're compliant and we're not. Computer networks are global, so not only do businesses and governments in our country need to be compliant but so do all those throughout the world.

Managers—and the general public—have been slow to understand the size and immediacy of the Y2K problem. A survey of Fortune 500 companies done in December 1997 revealed that 80 percent had not begun addressing the Y2K problem soon enough to have a reasonable chance of finishing on time. Another survey of 500 small businesses showed that only 41 percent were even addressing the problem at all.

THE IMPACT ON THE ECONOMY

Trying to estimate the economic impact of the Y2K problem, experts are offering their best guesses. *Business Week* commissioned a study in which the results predicted the U.S. economy will slow by a significant 0.3 per cent in 1999 and 0.5 percent in 2000 and 2001 because so many man-hours will be spent debugging instead of producing. The Federal Reserve Board has predicted the worldwide repair bill at about $300 billion. The Gartner Group, a consulting firm based in Stamford, Conn., predicts more catastrophic losses— in the neighborhood of $600 billion worldwide.

Possibly the biggest Y2K cost of all will be incurred after Jan 1, 2000, when systems begin to fail. This world will not be ready at the prescribed time and it's going to cause some economic damage and people are going to sue. Potential liabilities may develop with software companies whose products fail, with businesses who do not fulfill customer or client contracts accurately or on time, or even with accounting firms who neglect to adequately report companies not Y2K compliant incorporate audits.

As you can imagine, law firms must be drooling. They can hardly wait. The cost of suits resulting from failures is likely to exceed $1.5 trillion. This fallout of lawsuits and lost revenue from computer breakdowns may very likely create an unprecedented number of bankruptcies, which will lead to layoffs and skyrocketing unemployment. Both business and home foreclosures will probably hit a level not seen since the Great Depression.

Local and state governments who have recognized the problem are struggling to find enough funds to cover their Y2K costs. A year ago California estimated its Y2K costs at $50 million but recently upped it to $850 million. The federal government has gotten a late start (President Clinton created a White House panel in February 1998), and some sectors may not be ready. A subcommittee of the House Government Operations and Oversight Committee predicted that 37 percent of the federal government's computers will not be debugged in time. They could shut down, or if they keep working, they may provide inaccurate data. In a worst-case scenario, Social Security and other entitlement checks could be delayed for a significant period of time, leaving millions of Americans in economic distress.

Outside the United States, the situation is even worse. Much of the world is already in a serious economic recession. The Y2K crisis will just compound the problem. Europe is farther behind in addressing the Y2K problem than we are. Even now many businesses and governments have not even begun to make the needed corrections. Those who are, won't finish in time. Third World countries don't have the money or expertise to address the problem adequately.

When a Russian official was asked what his country was doing about the Y2K problem he answered, "We'll worry about that in the year 2000." I guess the reasoning is that they're too busy with economic and political problems right now to spend time and money worrying about the consequences of computer malfunctions in the future. In a world economy that is already struggling, ignoring the Y2K problem will bring disaster to some countries. And, as we all know, when one country's economy goes down, others will follow, and the United States will eventually be hit and hit hard. So, even if every computer in the U.S. were corrected in time, we will still feel the effects from abroad, and these effects can have serious economic consequences.

The Y2K bug is a global problem. Everyone will be having trouble at the same time. In a normal disaster—hurricane, power outage, etc.—you can rely on help from outside the disaster zone. But in this situation the disaster zone may be the entire industrialized world. There is no "outside."

WHAT YOU CAN DO TO PROTECT YOURSELF

Although no one can predict to what degree the Y2K bug will affect us. One thing we know for sure and that is it will have some effect. For some it will have a very significant effect simply because many businesses simply won't be prepared. Even if the Y2K bug doesn't cause much of a crisis, the worldwide recession, which is already raging, will.

What are you doing to prepare for the eventual problems that lie ahead? Troubled times lie ahead for those who are not prepared. Are you going to be ready? Will you be able to provide food, shelter, and other necessities of life when hard times come? That's what this book is about—how to prepare yourself financially and not only survive the financial crisis that is coming, but profit from it.

In this book, you will learn how to take advantage of the economic climate to make lots of money. In a time when job security is threatened, unemployment is on the rise, businesses are going into bankruptcy, and foreclosures skyrocketing, *you can become rich!*

This book will show you how to take advantage of bankruptcies, foreclosures, tax and estate sales, and cash in on the lucrative distressed properties market. With this knowledge you can literally become a millionaire in a short time! Many have already done it. If you start now, you can prepare for the hard times that lie ahead for everyone else. You will be able to live like a king when everyone else is struggling just to make ends meet. What you will learn in this book works in both good times and bad, but it's during recessions, like the one we are now facing, that the opportunities are best.

_2_

A GOLDEN OPPORTUNITY

ECONOMIC CHANGE BRINGS OPPORTUNITY

While most people are apprehensive about what the future may bring and what troubles may lie ahead, along with the trials will come fantastic opportunities for acquiring great wealth. Regardless of the cause, you can take advantage of the economic climate to cash in on an opportunity of a lifetime. Whenever the economy takes a nose dive, opportunity for financial gain arises, and the greater the crisis the greater the opportunity. You have a once-in-a-lifetime opportunity to cash in the biggest crisis this country has seen in 70 years. You can take advantage of it and enjoy rich financial rewards, or ignore it and suffer the painful consequences along with everyone else. The choice is yours.

Whenever economic troubles strike, business profits drop and unemployment rises. Raises are few and far between, some may have their salary cut. Many people are happy just to have a job. Economically depressed times, however, opens up an opportunity for those who are prepared. You can be one of these.

The worst economic crisis to hit this country, and in fact the world, was the Great Depression of the 1930s. Unemployment rates soared past 30 percent. Many banks and other businesses failed. Hundreds of thousands of people lost their jobs. Many former white collar workers ended up chopping wood or doing other types of manual labor just to survive. Foreclosures and bankruptcies were at an all time high. Despite the turmoil, we survived. After a few years, banks and other businesses blossomed again. Property values rose, the economy rose higher than it had ever before.

Recessions have occurred now and then, but the general overall path has been one of affluence and economic growth.

The biggest recession since the Great Depression occurred in the early 1980s. I was living in Houston, Texas at the time. The oil industry, which is a major part of the Houston economy, was one of the biggest hit. Tens of thousands of people were laid off. Businesses failed. Property values dropped. Foreclosures abounded.

In three years approximately 60,000 homes went into foreclosure, and this was in just the city of Houston. Similar rates were recorded in other cities around the country. In some neighborhoods nearly half of the homes went into foreclosure. Most of the homeowners walked away because of unemployment, lost investments, or other financial problems. Some simply picked up and left because their property value sunk lower than the amounts they owed on their loans. It wasn't unusual for a homeowner to buy a second home to take advantage of lower property values and interest rates and let the first house go into foreclosure.

A few enterprising individuals took advantage of the situation and began buying the glut of foreclosed properties at rock bottom prices and renting or reselling them at a huge profits. Many of these individuals became filthy rich.

I had a friend who was seriously considering walking out and leaving his home to the finance company. His loan balance was $70,000, but with decreasing property values his home was only worth $68,000. He bought the home for $76,000. He lost all his equity and now he owed the bank more than what it was worth. He had already missed one payment.

An investor came in and paid the back payments and assumed the loan and took possession of the deed to the property. The investor's total cost was about $1,600. He rented the home out for enough to pay the monthly mortgage plus a little more.

He kept the home for eight years, it didn't cost him anything because the rent paid for the mortgage and maintenance. As the economy improved property values increased. After eight years he sold the home for $102,000. He reaped a $32,000 profit! This investor probably had a string of homes he picked up during these lean years for next to nothing and was now cashing in. If he had bought only 10 homes and netted a similar profit he would have earned $320,000! Thirty homes would have provided him with a million dollars! By this time a light should be going on inside your head. Economic crises brings an abundance of foreclosed and distressed properties and along with it the opportunity to make big bucks! This example isn't even the best or the most profitable way to cash in on distressed and foreclosed properties. I will show you later how to acquire property without risking a cent of your own money and how you can turn around and resell the property almost immediately for a huge profit.

Not all homes that go into foreclosure are like the one I just described, where more is owed on mortgage than what the property is worth. I mentioned this example to show you that even in a worst case scenario you can still make a killing. Most of the homes you would look for will be valued much higher than the mortgage amount. This allows you the option to either rent the home or immediately resell for a quicker return on your investment.

There are many homes that are available through foreclosure and other means that can be turned around and resold almost immediately for profits as high as $10,000, $20,000, even $30,000.

A golden opportunity awaits you in the foreclosed and distressed properties market. The coming economic crash could be enormous, flooding the market with thousands of homes from which you can become financially independent.

Can you get rich buying and selling foreclosed properties? Yes! Very much so. Many people already have. Most have done it when the economic climate was relatively healthy and foreclosures few in number. But as economic turmoil hits, an abundance of homes will be available for not only you, but anyone else smart enough to cash in the this money making bonanza. Most millionaires acquired their wealth through real estate. It is the only sure investment you can possibly make. Putting money in the bank isn't a safe bet, as banks can fail. Putting money in the stock market isn't guaranteed, we all know it can collapse. But real estate is different from all the rest. It has its minor ups and downs, but the overall trend is up. That's what makes real estate such a good investment, even when values are depressed. Real estate always rebounds. On the average, real estate has always increased in value.

You don't need a lot of money to start investing in real estate. Properties can be obtained for a couple of thousand dollars and as little as a few hundred. In fact, there are properties you can pick up for less than $100. Sound incredible? It's done every day by those who know how to do it. You'll learn about it in this book.

IS IT ETHICAL?

One the beautiful things about this business is that it helps people. This may sound strange at first because buying foreclosed or distressed property at below market values sounds so good it seems unethical for some reason? You are profiting from someone else's misfortune. Well, that part is true, but you have no control over other people's problems. Even though you can benefit from other's misfortunes, you also provide a very worthwhile and valuable service to these people for which they are grateful.

Most homeowners don't know anything about the foreclosure process. As a consequence, after they've missed a few payments and have been threatened by their lender, they simply pack up their belongings and move out, leaving their home vacant. To them this seems to be the easiest way out of a financial dilemma. Those who try to do something find that lenders will refuse to discuss the matter or work with them. They demand full payment, partial payments being unacceptable. The homeowner may try to sell the property, but if they can find a buyer the buyer must get involved in the legal proceedings and must pay all missed payments and penalties. This scares most potential buyers away. The only option left for the struggling homeowner is to run away and let the home go into foreclosure. You can help the homeowner and at the same time earn a substantial profit.

What happens if the property goes into foreclosure? The house is taken away from the owner with no compensation whatsoever. The lender may even be able to come after the former owner to pay additional debts. His credit record is marred for seven years. That's how long foreclosures stay on credit reports.

Your efforts to buy foreclosed and distressed properties can be a blessing to those who are financially endangered. Never look at buying foreclosed or distressed property as cheap or dishonest, it is a very honorable thing that truly helps the homeowner. The only time when it can become cheap is when you take unfair advantage of a homeowner and do not offer a reasonable exchange for the property. Sometimes a reasonable exchange is simply taking over the mortgage with no additional payment involved. You will learn more about this later.

HOW TO GET RICH

Doubled My Money

My first exposure in buying real estate was in the foreclosure market back in the 1970s when I was a college student. During the summer I worked in a manufacturing plant. My supervisor had been buying homes fixing them up and reselling or renting them. He became so successful that he quite his job to devote full-time to his real estate investment business.

Inspired by his success, two fellow workers and I pooled our money to try our hand at the foreclosure market. We chose to try our hand with foreclosures because it didn't require much money to obtain the properties and we didn't have much. We all worked for less than $3 an hour so we didn't have much capital to work with. I contributed $1,000, essentially my life savings. Our total amounted to $3,500. With this amount of money in hand we went out to seek our fortune in real estate. What I learned from that experience was astounding. We were three novices, college aged kids with no real estate knowledge to speak of. The odds seemed to be against us.

At the foreclosure auction we had our eyes on one particular house. We had looked it over earlier. It was a two bedroom home, two years old in a decent neighborhood. There were only two other bidders present. The opening bid was $3,000, the amount the lender needed to satisfy accumulated expenses. We bid $3,100. Another person bid $3,200. We upped the bid to $3,300. He bid $3,400. We countered with $3500, the entire amount we had to work with. The other bidder remained silent. The auctioneer called out $3,500 going once...$3500 going twice...sold for $3,500. In a matter of minutes three naive college students became owners of a home valued at near

$45,000. We paid the cashier the money and took over the loan of the property. It was that simple.

The home needed a little yard work and a little paint, which we did. We sold it within a three months. My total cash outlay was $1,500 (the additional $500 was for material to fix the house and to pay mortgage during the time we owned it). We sold the house to pay off the original loan and expenses, leaving us with a little over $10,000. My share of the profit was $3,000—a 200 percent profit in three months! We were on to something. I doubled my money in three months. I don't know of any investment that could come close to matching this.

I was surprised how simple it was to acquire foreclosed property and then turn around and resell it for a handsome profit. We didn't need to be financial wizards to pull this off. It was easy.

Although that experience showed me the potential of investing in foreclosed property, I only did it as a short term experiment and went on to pursue my college studies.

Retired At 55

After college my interest in real estate was again renewed when I purchased my own home. One of my colleagues had become involved in real estate investing. He was always telling me of the great deals he was getting in both buying and selling. He was making so much money from his real estate deals that when he turned 55 he announced he was retiring. I asked him why he was giving up a $56,000 a year job and taking early retirement, which would give him only a fraction of his salary. To me it seemed like he was letting go of a good deal of financial security. His answer to me was, "I have to quit, with my real estate investments, I'm making too much money!" He retired 10 years early and with his dealings in real estate made a comfortable living.

The Time is Now

My interest in real estate was renewed. It was 1984, the economy sprung a leak and the real estate market was sinking like the Titanic. My enthusiasm for getting involved was severely hampered by the poor economic climate. I was a fool because I didn't do anything. This was a time when opportunity for making a killing was at its height. In the city of Houston where I lived, foreclosures were occurring at a rate of 2,500 a month. This huge influx of unwanted properties provided a gold mine for savvy real estate investors to pick up property for almost nothing.

Thousands of homes passes through foreclosure auctions. There were far more homes than there were buyers. Anyone could have made a killing. Not all property sold at these foreclosure sales were a bargain and just gong to the auctions did not mean a person could pick up a good deal. But if you did your homework, you couldn't miss out on the many bargains constantly available.

About 5 percent of the homes in the United States go into foreclosure during serious recessions. That's a lot of real estate. Even in good economic times about 1 percent of homes are threatened with foreclosure. So, the market for foreclosed properties is a good investment in both good and bad times.

I stood idly by while homes went into foreclosure all around me. I could have jumped in and bought properties while I had a good job, and either kept them as investment property or resold them for a profit. Even though I had experimented in the foreclosure market earlier, I didn't really realize the potential during this time of economic turmoil.

I didn't get involved in foreclosures again until I was a victim myself. It was then that I started to really study real estate and foreclosures. I was facing the possibility of having my home taken away. I searched every avenue I could, to avoid losing my home. My mortgage company refused to help me and I was forced to search in other directions. In my search to save my home from foreclosure I uncovered a wealth of information. I was led into the world of real estate investing, a world unknown to the general public.

My home lost value. I bought the house for $74,000 but my home was worth only about $64,000. I considered walking away. In my search to save my home I discovered how to use foreclosure to my benefit and turned this $10,000 loss in depreciation into a $48,000 gain.

I not only learned about the lucrative foreclosure market, but I discovered the even more lucrative market of buying and selling distressed properties. With distressed property you can get unbelievable bargains well below current market values. Distressed properties are those that are owned by people who are having serious financial problems. They've stopped paying their mortgage, and are facing the possibility of losing their homes although, not yet officially in foreclosure. To get out from under this mess they are willing to sell or even walk out of their homes if they have to, just to get away.

You can buy these properties from the owners, before they go into foreclosure for only a few hundred dollars in may cases. Some investors have been able to get possession of property for absolutely nothing! That's right, the investor, in essence, promises to take over the mortgage and save the former owner from the foreclosure and thus save his credit record. This is not rare, but admittedly deals like this are not found every day. More typically a payment of $500 to $1,000 would be made. The homes are then turned around and resold for profits ranging from $10,000 to $20,000 and more.

How do you find these bargains? That's what you will find out in later chapters. Locating prime foreclosed and distressed properties that can be purchased at prices substantially below their market value.

This book is a result of the discoveries I made and opens up to everybody the fantastic opportunities that await those who are not afraid to take a chance of getting rich in real estate.

BUY LOW, SELL HIGH

What is the secret to success in any business or investment? The key to financial success is summed up in these few immortal words "buy low and sell high." If you follow this advice you are on the right path to financial wealth. This often repeated quip has been used as a humorous solution to business success, but in reality the statement is absolutely true and is the key to success in any business, including real estate investment.

The prevailing philosophy in real estate investment has been to buy property and hold onto it. Rent it out, using that income to pay for the mortgage and maintenance, and if you are lucky you might even make a small profit. It really doesn't matter if you make much with this because in time the property will appreciate in value. Eventually, 10 or 15 years in the future you will sell the property for a profit. This philosophy is still widely advocated. The only problem with this technique is that it takes 10 to 15 years to not only make a profit, but to get your original investment back.

Even if you spent only $2,000 in closing costs and a down payment for each property, you would be locking up a lot of money as you started to acquire more and more real estate.

The philosophy in this book is to buy and resell as quickly as possible. Although buying property and renting it out for a time may be wise in certain circumstances, your ultimate goal should be to sell as quickly as you can. Use the profit you earn from that transaction to bankroll your next, and your next, steamrolling you into a position of financial freedom. Your profit for each transaction may be smaller, but you will be able to do it more often. That's the way to make money in real estate.

In order to buy and sell property quickly for a substantial profit, you need to located real estate that is undervalued to begin with. The cheapest real estate you will ever find is foreclosed and distressed property. Not only are they often undervalued, but you can pick them up without risking much of your own capital. Many properties can be obtained for almost nothing. Once you learn how to acquire these properties you can put the saying "buy low , sell high" to work for you to accumulate a great deal of wealth.

In this book you will not only learn about buying and selling foreclosed real estate, but you will also learn how to acquire personal property such as household appliances, office equipment, sporting goods, furniture, automobiles, and jewelry for pennies on the dollar. All these items coming from personal and business bankruptcies. These items can be acquired for your own use or sold for handsome profits. Many businesses make their living off buying and selling merchandise this way. You can do the same.

3

THE FORECLOSURE PROCESS

Bob Garraway and his wife Susan were sold on the new $80,000 house; it seemed to fit all their needs. They had been looking for several months before finding this one. It was none too soon for Bob; interest rates had been skyrocketing for the previous two years, and he felt lucky to lock into a deal with an interest rate of 15 percent. While this may sound high, in 1981, when the Garraways purchased their home, interest rates were predicted, by all those that knew anything about real estate (and even by those who didn't), to shoot up past 20 percent. At such rates Bob and Susan would be unable to afford a home. Buying when they did got them into a house before rates soared out of reach.

The Garraways put $8,000 down on the home and agreed to make mortgage payments of $900 a month. Bob had a good paying job with a large engineering firm. When he joined the company in 1980, he was told that he could expect regular salary increases and many benefits. His technical skills were in high demand and he enjoyed a comfortable income.

When the recession hit in 1982, Bob wasn't worried. Like most people, he felt that it was only a minor inconvenience that would be over soon. This wasn't the case, however, gradually he saw friends and fellow employees lose their jobs. His company cut back its personnel and its benefits. By 1985 Bob found himself standing in the unemployment line with hundreds of others. He had lived in his home for four years and had sunk thousands of dollars into mortgage payments and upkeep.

Without a job, it became increasingly difficult for Bob to keep up his monthly payments. Eventually he had to make a decision to let the mortgage payments slip by unpaid.

The bank that held the mortgage on the Garraway's home sent them letters threatening foreclosure. They demanded all back payments plus late fees and refused to accept anything but full payment.

Without a job and with no immediate prospect of finding one, Bob felt that only one road was open to him. Packing up their bags, the Garraways left their home and what equity they had in it. Soon thereafter the bank foreclosed on their property and sold it at a foreclosure auction. The Garraways lost everything, or so it seemed: no home, no job, no money. They were left only with mental scars that would last a lifetime.

This story has been repeated many times across the country for countless numbers of unfortunate people. It will occur many times more in the future. At the present time, about three million homes in the United States are facing foreclosure. In addition, statistics reveal that another nine and a half million homeowners are delinquent in their payments. For many the outlook is bleak.

Bob and Susan Garraway did what thousands of people have done and are still doing—walking away from their homes freely giving them up to their lenders and destroying their credit. Yet, in almost all cases they could have cut their losses and saved their credit.

Reasons for falling behind in mortgage payments vary and are often unpredictable. They include: loss of job, illness, accident, lawsuit, bad debts, rising taxes and utility rates, divorce, or weak real estate prices which keep owners from selling. Non-payment of homeowner's insurance premiums is another cause for concern. Lenders have the right to foreclose if the homeowner doesn't keep adequate insurance coverage on their home.

People may also be threatened with the loss of their home by the government. Failure to pay property taxes, school tax, and other taxes, or even utility bills will bring the local government after you. The government can foreclose on a home in spite of the lenders. Since lenders want to protect their investment, many of them require that homeowners pay real estate taxes along with their mortgage payments. The tax money is then set aside in an escrow account. Each month a little more is added to this account so that when the taxes become due there will be sufficient funds to pay for them in a lump sum.

At the end of the year, taxes can build up to as much as a couple of thousand dollars. If the homeowner has not been budgeting for this expense, he may find himself coming up short and facing foreclosure from the local government, something neither the homeowner nor the lender wants. If the

taxes are paid with the mortgage payment, the lender can be sure these obligations will be met.

UNDERSTANDING FORECLOSURE

Foreclosure represents the termination of all rights the mortgagor (the homeowner) has in property covered by the mortgage or deed of trust. In short, the mortgagee (the lender) has full legal power to repossess the home. When the debtor fails to make payment, the property is confiscated and sold at an auction so that the lender may recapture his investment.

The laws governing foreclosure vary from state to state and are subject to terms contained in the mortgage document itself. All foreclosures take time and are subject to a strict set of legal requirements. The mortgagee cannot foreclose on someone overnight. In most cases homeowners are given ample time to make up payments. Initially his major thrust will be to scare homeowners into resuming payments. In most cases the lender does not want to foreclose if he doesn't have to. This is especially true when the economy is sluggish and the lender has more property on his hands than he can handle. Mortgage payments are his bread and butter; foreclosing interrupts the flow of money into his pockets. In general, foreclosure is more costly than it is beneficial to the lender.

Don't believe that if the homeowner has missed a mortgage payment all is lost and the only solution is to run away. Abandoning a home is the biggest mistake anyone facing foreclosure can make. Homeowners are given several months in order to tackle the problem before they are actually forced to move. In some cases, especially when there are many foreclosures occurring, lenders can take a year or more, but they may also complete the process in as little as six months. The actual time depends on several factors, but the sooner you begin working to acquire a property the better.

The speed in which the foreclosure process runs its course is very important to you as an investor. In order to stop the process and acquire the property at the cheapest possible price you need to work fast. Once the home has gone too far the only way to acquire the property is at a foreclosure auction where you may have competition and where expenses will be greater. Knowing the type of security device (mortgage or deed or trust) used on the property will help you gauge the time you have. The following section discusses the differences in some detail.

SECURITY DEVICES

Jason worked in construction in California where he lived. His brother Chuck had the same type of work in Illinois. During a recent economic recession both Jason and Chuck were laid off. New employment was not readily available. With unemployment compensation running out and no sign of financial relief, Jason and Chuck each became delinquent on their mortgage payments.

Jason's lender foreclosed on his home after six months of nonpayment. Chuck on the other hand, remained at his residence for a full 18 months before he was forced to leave. Why was Chuck able to stay in his home 12 months longer than Jason? What was the difference? Many factors could have influenced the time involved. Each lender is different, and the length of time a person may stay in a home can depend on the lender's attitude toward foreclosures. Other factors include: the amount of equity in the home, type of loan, current real estate market, location, and the lender's current needs or wants. One of the major differences, however, is the type of security device on the property. The laws in each state determine to a great extent the type of security the lender can hold and consequently the amount of time required to repossess a home in default. The mortgage is what everyone refers to in regards to paying off a home loan. But just what is a mortgage? Not all so-called mortgages are true mortgages.

Mortgages

Few people have enough cash on hand to walk in and buy a new home outright. The typical home today sells in the neighborhood of $100,000, a huge sum to most of us. If it weren't for the fact that we could buy on credit, few people could afford a home without accumulating years of savings.

To buy a house without having the ready cash, the prospective home buyer must borrow the money from a lending institution such as a bank or a mortgage company. With this money he can then purchase the house from the present owner.

In order for the bank to lend money to the new home buyer, the buyer has to put up some collateral as security. All lenders require some sort of security device in case of default by the borrower. What the home buyer provides is called a mortgage. With a mortgage the homeowner (mortgagor) pledges the title of the house and land (real property) as security to the lender (mortgagee). In the event that the mortgagor does not meet his payment obligations and defaults on the loan, the mortgagee can repossess the property. It is then sold at a foreclosure auction to recoup the amount loaned.

The homeowner holds the title to the property when the mortgage is taken out. The lender who decides to take possession of the home must take court action, potentially a long and involved process lasting as much as a year.

Because of the complexity and difficulty of gaining possession of homes, a newer form of security for home financing has been created by lenders. A failure on the part of the homeowner to keep up payments can lead to a much quicker eviction and loss of property than with the mortgage. This new type of security, called a *deed of trust*, originated on the West Coast and spread rapidly across the country.

Deed of Trust

The deed of trust, also called a trust deed or a mortgage note is, strictly speaking, not a mortgage. It serves the same purpose as a mortgage by allowing the lender to take possession of the property if the homeowner becomes delinquent on payments. Trust deeds contain an additional clause referred to as the *power of sale*. This allows the lender (actually the trustee) to take possession of the home without the trouble of going to court as required by a traditional mortgage. Technically, foreclosure under a deed of trust can occur in just a couple of months.

With a mortgage there are only two parties involved, the mortgagee and the mortgagor. With a trust deed there are three parties, the beneficiary (lender), the trustor (borrower), and the trustee (stake holder). The new face is the trustee and is independent of both the lender and the borrower. The trustee can be a title company, an escrow company, or a trust company specifically set up to function as the trustee. The purpose of the trustee is to be the stake holder or deed holder. If the homeowner defaults on the loan, title of the property is conveyed to the trustee, who then sells it and pays the lender the portion due on the unpaid balance of the loan.

In California, where the deed of trust is most commonly used, a house can be put up for sale only ninety days after a notice of default is filed. In some cases this time can even be shorter. The homeowner can stop the sale only by paying off the entire amount of the loan, plus interest.

Once a lender has delivered a notice of default and accelerated the due date on the loan, the total amount of the loan becomes due. There are ways to get around this, however, which I will discuss in later chapters.

The term "mortgage" has been used for so many years that most people, including real estate agents and lenders, commonly refer to a trust deed as a mortgage. To keep things simple, I will follow the trend and generally will refer to both mortgages and trust deeds as mortgages. I will also call the homeowner "the mortgagor" and the lender "the mortgagee". If a distinction between the two is necessary, I will clarify.

TYPES OF FORECLOSURE

The state government dictates which type of security device lenders are permitted to use. In some states such as Arkansas, Kentucky, and Maryland, both are required. The chart on page 14 shows the predominant type of security and method of foreclosure for each state.

FORECLOSURE PROCEDURE BY STATE

This table lists only the predominant method of foreclosure used in each state. Most states use more than one method of foreclosure. You will need to refer to the foreclosure law citations listed in Appendix A to find detailed information.

State	Predominant Security Device	Predominant Foreclosure Method	Redemption Period	Possession During Redemption
Alabama	Mortgage	Power of Sale	1 Year	Buyer
Alaska	Trust Deed	Power of Sale	None	-
Arizona	Trust Deed	Power of Sale	None	-
Arkansas	Mortgage	Power of Sale	1 Year	Buyer
California	Trust Deed	Power of Sale	None	-
Colorado	Trust Deed	Power of Sale	75 Days	Mortgagor
Connecticut	Mortgage	Strict Foreclosure	None	-
Delaware	Mortgage	Judicial	None	-
Washington D.C.	Trust Deed	Power of Sale	None	-
Florida	Mortgage	Judicial	10 Days	-
Georgia	Mortgage	Power of Sale	None	-
Hawaii	Trust Deed	Power of Sale	None	-
Idaho	Trust Deed	Power of Sale	None	-
Illinois	Mortgage	Judicial	1 Year	Mortgagor
Indiana	Mortgage	Judicial	3 Months	Mortgagor
Iowa	Mortgage	Judicial	6 Months	Mortgager
Kansas	Mortgage	Judicial	1 Year	Mortgagor
Kentucky	Mortgage	Judicial	None	-
Louisiana	Mortgage	Judicial	None	-
Maine	Mortgage	Entry & Possession	1 Year	Mortgagor
Maryland	Trust Deed	Power of Sale	None	-
Massachusetts	Mortgage	Power of Sale	None	-
Michigan	Mortgage	Power of Sale	6 Months	Mortgagor
Minnesota	Mortgage	Power of Sale	6 Months	Mortgagor
Mississippi	Trust Deed	Power of Sale	None	-
Missouri	Trust Deed	Power of Sale	1 Year	Mortgagor
Montana	Mortgage	Judicial	None	-
Nebraska	Mortgage	Judicial	None	-
Nevada	Mortgage	Power of Sale	None	-
New Hampshire	Mortgage	Power of Sale	None	-
New Jersey	Mortgage	Judicial	10 Days	-
New Mexico	Mortgage	Judicial	1 Month	Buyer
New York	Mortgage	Judicial	None	-
North Carolina	Trust Deed	Power of Sale	None	-
North Dakota	Mortgage	Judicial	1 Year	Mortgagor
Ohio	Mortgage	Judicial	None	-
Oklahoma	Mortgage	Judicial	None	-
Oregon	Trust Deed	Power of Sale	None	-
Pennsylvania	Mortgage	Judicial	None	-
Rhode Island	Mortgage	Power of Sale	None	-
South Carolina	Mortgage	Judicial	None	-
South Dakota	Mortgage	Power of Sale	1 Year	Mortgagor
Tennessee	Trust Deed	Power of Sale	None	-
Texas	Trust Deed	Power of Sale	None	-
Utah	Mortgage	Judicial	6 Months	Mortgagor
Vermont	Mortgage	Strict Foreclosure	6 Months	Mortgagor
Virginia	Trust Deed	Power of Sale	None	-
Washington	Mortgage	Judicial	1 Year	Buyer
West Virginia	Trust Deed	Power of Sale	None	-
Wisconsin	Mortgage	Power of Sale	None	-
Wyoming	Mortgage	Power of Sale	6 Months	Mortgagor

With a mortgage (as opposed to a trust deed) the lender must go to court to get possession of your property. Going through the courts is a long, involved process and may take as much as a year before the matter is settled. States such as Connecticut and Vermont, which use mortgages, have what is known as strict foreclosures. The lender must still go to court to take the property, but the process is streamlined to move more rapidly.

With a deed of trust, the lender can move in even faster since no court action is required. All he must do is simply send the homeowner a notice and advertise the sale in the newspaper. Within just weeks after receiving the notice of default, the home could be sold. A sobering thought. It is no wonder most lenders will use trust deeds if not restricted by state regulations.

Even more terrifying than a foreclosure under the trust deed is an entry foreclosure. Maine, Connecticut, Vermont, and New Hampshire all use entry foreclosures under certain circumstances. Although these are mortgage states, the mortgagee can foreclose by evicting the mortgagor and taking possession of the property without going to court.

THE STEPS TOWARD FORECLOSURE

Knowing what steps are involved in a foreclosure will help you understand the process more clearly and help you in dealing with lenders and financially troubled homeowners.

Knowing whether the homeowner has a deed of trust or a mortgage will give you a handle on the amount of time to expect before the lender formally forecloses on the property.

If a person has a mortgage (as opposed to a trust deed) he can, with few exceptions, be foreclosed on only through a court action. Just to have the lender tell him he's in default and that his home will soon be repossessed, is not enough. He has the legal right to remain in the home until a court decides in favor of the lender.

Foreclosures take time. Even with a deed of trust, which needs no court action, an eviction will take at least three or four months. This is a minimum you can generally expect, usually it will take longer, sometimes much longer. Retaining possession of a home for a year is not unusual, even with a trust deed.

If a lender is dead set on taking someone's property for some reason, he can speed the foreclosure by processing his paperwork faster. Even so, it still must go through legal channels that slow down the operation. Most lenders are not in any hurry to foreclose on anyone because foreclosure generally means a loss of income for them. It means all hope of the homeowner resuming payments is gone, and he must now get rid of unwanted real estate by selling it at auction. This could be costly and time consuming for him.

Any lender, if not overworked with a swarm of other foreclosures, will speed up the process if a house is left vacant. Empty houses encourage vandalism, which decreases property value. A house that is occupied usually remains in livable condition because at least yard work is kept up. The homeowner has a right to remain in his home until the property is either repossessed or sold at a foreclosure auction.

Warning Letters

Once a payment is missed, the first thing the lender will do is send a warning letter or past due notice. This is only a past due notice and not a notice that foreclosure is in progress. The content of these letters vary from one lender to the next, but they are all designed to worn the homeowner of possible loss of the home if payment isn't sent immediately. The homeowner is instructed to send in the full previous month's payment plus a late fee, which amounts to an additional four to five percent of the monthly payment.

This letter is just a warning, and is meant to encourage the homeowner to continue making payments. In many cases the missed payment may have been an oversight, and the homeowner quickly pays it. In other cases the homeowner has run low on money and is unable to make the payment on time, but makes it up as soon as possible. These warning letters motivate payment out of fear of losing the home.

When the second month rolls around and payment is not received, another past due notice is sent. It may sound even more threatening than the first. Payment for the past two months plus penalties will be demanded, and the letter may state that no partial payments will be accepted.

A mortgage is considered "delinquent" when any payment is not made by its due date. It is in "default" when two or more payments are missed. Most mortgage contracts allow foreclosure to begin when a default exists, but lenders are generally not so impatient. They want to give the mortgagor full opportunity to catch up on delinquent payments.

Government insured loans from the FHA and VA, require a minimum of three delinquent months before foreclosure proceedings can commence. Banks and other lenders generally follow suit. Some time after the second or third month after becoming delinquent, the homeowner can expect to receive a notice of default. With this notice, foreclosure is technically commencing. In actual practice, this is not always true.

Notice of Default

When the lender realizes that the homeowner has completely stopped paying on his mortgage and will make no satisfactory effort to pay, he sends a notice of default. This notice in effect is saying that the loan is being accelerated or in other words, the lender is demanding immediate payment of the full amount of the loan. It also indicates that notice is being recorded at the county recorder's office that the homeowner is in foreclosure. Because the notice has been filed at the county recorder's office, the foreclosure now becomes a matter of public record. In a mortgage state, the lender will file a lawsuit at the same time.

In most cases, the lender does not want to repossess the house; he would rather receive regular payments. For this reason, the notice of default is rarely sent until after at least three months delinquency. In times when there are many foreclosures and the workload is heavy, it may take even longer; up to a year or more is possible.

No matter how many letters the lender has sent and regardless what the letters may say, the homeowner is not officially in foreclosure until he has received a notice of default and the notice is filed and recorded in the county courthouse. This notice, will state "Notice of Default" and will indicate that the property is in foreclosure. It may even state the number of months remaining to make up payments before the house is put up for sale.

This notice is usually sent by certified mail, which means that it has to be signed for when it's delivered to the homeowner. Some people, knowing this, try to forestall foreclosure by simply refusing to accept the letter. If not accepted, the letter is sent back stamped "unclaimed" or "refused". This tactic will not work. As long as the letter has been delivered to the last known address, it satisfies all legal requirements. They will gain no extra time and foreclosure will proceed as scheduled.

Once a notice of default has been sent, it may take another three months or so to process, if a trust deed is involved. A mortgage will take a little longer. Give or take a month or two, it commonly takes about six months before a foreclosure sale occurs.

If the homeowner happens to have a low interest loan that's below the current rate, he's especially vulnerable to foreclosure. Some lenders are eager to remove any low interest loans from their books and resell at a higher rate. Banks and other lending institutions make their profits from the interest rates they charge. Even a half percent difference in the interest rate can mean many thousands of dollars to them over the life of the loan. For this reason, anyone who defaults on a loan with an interest rate below the current rate will be a prime target for a speedy foreclosure.

In a trust deed state, if the lender wants to get hold of a property badly enough he can serve a notice of default and begin foreclosure the first two or three months after the property becomes delinquent. Paperwork can be processed in just a few weeks, cutting the entire operation down to less than four months. Although possible, fortunately for the homeowner this is not common.

Notice of Sale

When the foreclosure process has run its course, the homeowner will receive a letter informing him that the house will be sold, or rather put up for public auction. At the same time, the lender will have a notice posted at the courthouse announcing the sale. This will be done about three weeks before the auction because the mortgagee will be required to run an ad in the local paper for this length of time before the sale. The homeowner then has three weeks time from the receipt of the notification of the sale to vacate the house.

Once the notice of default has been sent, the foreclosure process is in its final stages, but it is still not too late for the homeowner to sell his home or reclaim it later. Most states allow homeowners a redemption period where they can make up all missed payments (plus late penalties and legal fees) and keep possession of the property. If the homeowner makes no attempt to save the house, it will be sold at auction at the appointed time. The redemption period can vary greatly between states. It can be 30, 60, 90 days, or as little as 10 days. Some states don't have any recognized redemption period, while others may allow up to a full year or more. (You will need to check the laws in your state. See the table on page 26 and Appendix A)

The auction is conducted by the county sheriff or by a referee or master appointed by the judge, and is commonly referred to as a sheriff's auction. It will usually be held either at the courthouse or on the property in question.

After the property is sold, the money received will go to the lender to pay off the mortgage balance and foreclosure fees. If there is any money left over after this, the debtor will be allowed to keep it. Unless the owner had a healthy amount of equity in the home, it is unlikely that the house will sell for a high enough price to allow any excess to pass to the former owner. In most cases the house will sell below its current market value. When this happens the former owner stands to lose most or all of his equity.

CONSEQUENCES OF FORECLOSURE

Loss of Property and Self Respect

The most apparent, and perhaps devastating, result of a foreclosure is that the homeowner loses property he has lived in, worked for, kept up and repaired for years. The family is literally forced out of what was once their home. Now, they are forced to evacuate without any compensation.

Hopes and dreams are ended, all they are left with is memories. It can be a dramatic emotional experience, as well as humiliating one, as they may perceive that others will look at them as deadbeats.

If they vacate the property before the foreclosure process is completed, they can avoid additional problems. Wherever they move they will have to report their former address and there will be a credit check. If the foreclosure has not be processed and reported yet, this will not show up on the credit report and there will be little problem in renting elsewhere. If a foreclosure is indicated there may be some difficulty in moving into a new residence as well as embarrassment explaining the situation.

Some families are forcibly removed from their homes if they continue to remain in them once the foreclosure sale is over. If they stay in their home this long, they risk losing *all* assets remaining on the property. The sheriff's deputies will evict them on the spot and confiscate all their property—furniture, appliances, bedding, toys, even the trash. The family would be lucky to escape with the car. This can be a devastating experience.

Some homeowners, refuse to accept reality and may not believe they are actually experiencing a foreclosure and try to remain in their home. Doing so, only makes matters worse because they risk losing not only the home, but everything they own. It is important that homeowners who are facing foreclosure realize these harsh facts and take steps immediately to resolve their problem with as little pain and embarrassment as possible.

An investor can help to solve the problems these homeowners face. More will be covered on this topic in Chapter 6.

How Foreclosure Affects Credit

What happens to a person's credit report after a foreclosure? Foreclosures remain on credit records for seven years. After seven years all bad credit references are wiped away, so to speak, except for bankruptcy which remains on for ten years.

A bad credit report can cause a great deal of trouble. When applying for a car loan, a business loan, or credit cards, credit references are checked. If there is a bad debt, the potential lender can, and often will, deny credit.

Getting a loan from another institution will depend on what type of credit is being sought and the creditor's attitude toward the situation. Any unfavorable entry in the credit report will make creditors more cautious about giving credit.

Before the mid 1980s, many mortgage lenders generally didn't bother to report bad debts to the credit bureau. Nowadays, lenders are using all the leverage they can to discourage people from packing their bags and leaving.

The FHA is requiring lenders in certain parts of the country to report foreclosures to at least one national credit reporting agency. The Federal National Mortgage Association (FNMA) also requires all of its 3800 approved mortgage lenders to report foreclosures and even loans which have been in default over 90 days. These steps have greatly increase the number of reported foreclosures.

Deficiency Judgments

Tarnishing a credit record is bad enough, but it is not the worst thing that can happen. A homeowner who has gone through foreclosure may also be hit with a deficiency judgment and owe the lender money in addition to the house.

In many cases the lender will not dispose of the property for enough to satisfy debts owed by the former homeowner. This possibility is one that can be of great concern to the homeowner. If the amount received is not enough to cover these expenses, the former homeowner will be required to pay the difference, an amount that often exceeds several thousand dollars!

If $60,000 is owed on a loan and the house sells at the foreclosure auction for only $50,000, the homeowner can be sued for the remaining $10,000, plus expenses. The lender may be able to collect personal assets, such as car, furniture, and savings, in order to recoup his losses. Occurrences such as this have perpetuated the fear of foreclosure among homeowners. However, fear of deficiency judgments in most cases is no longer justified.

Many states have laws which restrict lenders in what recourse they can take; this is particularly true when the property is secured with a deed of trust. For instance, if a house sells for a depressed price at a foreclosure auction, the lender may not be allowed the full difference between the selling price and the amount still owed on the loan. Instead a judgment may be given only for the difference between the court's appraised value of the property and the loan balance. In a severely depressed real estate climate where the home may sell at a price below the loan amount, the price received may be judged the fair market value and it would be hopeless for the lender to try to obtain a deficiency judgment. Laws like this pressure lenders to get the highest possible price they can, preventing them from unloading the property quickly and seeking a judgment.

Several states such as California, Montana, North Carolina, and North Dakota do not allow deficiency judgments at all in cases involving foreclosure. Judgments are also not allowed when the property has been reclaimed through a strict foreclosure.

In situations where a deed of trust is involved, the lender will likely open the bidding himself with a minimum bid equal to the outstanding loan amount. If anyone bids higher than this, the lender gets all his investment back. If no one else bids, he becomes the highest bidder and gets the home from the trustee who is selling it, and the loan is satisfied. The lender then will turn around and try to sell the property through ordinary channels.

In the past, it was rare for the lending institution to file suit to recoup the loan difference. In most cases, the former homeowner defaulted on the loan because of severe financial difficulties, in which case the court would be hard pressed to squeeze money out of him. When the debtor has been through some hard times and has lost his home, the court more than likely will let him off the hook. Bankers know this and although they legally have the right to sue, they rarely win such judgments. For this reason, we haven't seen many deficiency judgments go to court in the past.

With the onslaught of foreclosures in slow economic times this situation is slowly changing. Some people see foreclosure as a way to slip out of a poor financial situation. If the lender has reason to believe that the former homeowner was fully capable of continuing monthly mortgage payments and still meet other credit obligations, he will not hesitate to sue. Deficiency judgments are becoming more and more frequent all the time.

Many people who purchased a home with high interest rates when the economy was booming found themselves paying a high rate of interest on property that was decreasing in value.

Numerous homeowners in this situation escaped from the problem by simply packing up their bags and moving out, leaving the house for the lender to handle. Even though not confronted with a loss of work or other hardship, they saw foreclosure as a means to get out of a bad financial obligation. Some of these people found themselves facing deficiency judgments or a lawsuits from their lenders.

If the lender has reason to believe that a homeowner skipped out on his mortgage obligation just to avoid paying on a bad investment, and if the state allows deficiency judgments, a suit will most likely be filed.

Some homeowners have deliberately defaulted on their loans and walked away just so they could buy a new house at a cheaper price and lower interest rate. In this case, the lender can file a collection lawsuit against the defaulter. You can bet that if the lender suspects that a homeowner defaulted on his mortgage without good cause, he will sue, no matter what state he lives in. The fact that a suit hasn't been filed after the original house has been sold at a foreclosure auction does not mean they're off the hook either; lenders generally have four years to file a claim.

Mortgage insurance firms are the ones who most often sue for deficiency judgments. They mean business. Often it is the mortgage insurance firm that will sue because it is the mortgage insurance company that took the loss from a foreclosure.

If a person is sued for a deficiency judgment, he can't just ignore it by claiming not to have the money to pay. This would be the typical response, but that doesn't matter. The judgment will hang over their heads for years until payment is made and they will not be able to buy or sell any other property until it is taken care of.

The attorney for the lender or insurance firm files an abstract with the county clerk that lasts for 10 years. The abstract means the anytime the person attempts to buy or sell property in the county, the deal is frozen because of the debt owed. If the lender is particularly aggressive he can file one of those abstracts in most major cities, although that is unlikely.

So, if anyone believes that nothing bad can come of foreclosures, they're wrong. A judgment can mess up a person's life indefinitely. When the abstract expires at the end of 10 years, the lender can refile it for another 10.

Some lenders file suits en masse, then recording the abstracts, with the hopes that someday, somehow, they will get some money out of it. It is looked at by these insurance companies and lenders almost like an annuity that has a small up-front fee, but may pay off years in the future.

To decide who gets sued and who doesn't, lenders sometimes pick through foreclosures to find people they think may have some money. They look at your salary and the likelihood that you are still gainfully employed. Some companies are not so picky and sue everyone they can.

Most lenders and insurance companies pay lawyers on some kind of contingency fee. That is, the lawyers only get paid if they get some money out of the debtor. That can result in a lawyer probing around for non-exempt assets or a constable coming to the door asking for money.

All in all, a foreclosure can haunt the homeowner. The fact that lenders are sometimes slow to aggressively file collection suits doesn't subtract from the fact much. The drastic results of a foreclosure can linger for a long time.

4

HOW TO BUY FORECLOSED PROPERTY

REAL ESTATE BARGAINS

I hear 40 thousand, who will make it 55,000? Do I hear 55,000? . . . Fifty thousand going once, going twice, SOLD to the man over there for $50,000.

Would you like the thrill of buying a home appraised for $100,000, or more, for half its market value? If you're looking for a home or investment property, such a buy would be a steal. Is it even possible?

"It's all a dream," you might say. "This type of thing is only mentioned in hyped up 'get rich quick' books and is not factual." Baloney, it happens all the time, every day in fact. But in order to get the best deals you have to know where to look. Not knowing the secret of how to find the bargains prevents most buyers from getting the deals real estate investors have bragged about.

For investors, the foreclosure market provides a quick avenue to wealth. Andrew Carnegie, founder of U.S. Steel, once said "Ninety percent of all millionaires become so by owning real estate." The most lucrative area in the real estate market today is in foreclosed and distressed properties. As much as 50,000 properties go into foreclosure nationwide each month! This number will increase greatly in coming years. Are you prepared to take advantage of this golden opportunity?

You can cut yourself in on a piece of the pie through buying foreclosed and distressed properties. Whether you are simply looking for an inexpensive home to live in or a string of investment properties, the time to get good deals (and sometimes unbelievable deals) is here and it will get even better.

Thousands of homes and investment properties are foreclosed on each year. Statistically speaking, 1 percent of the homes in the United States suffer a foreclosure. In bad economic times this figure has jumped up to 5 percent. Some parts of the country suffer greater than others, and has been as high as 20 percent. In some areas during recent recessions, thousands of homes would go in foreclosure each month. In some neighborhoods literally half of the homes have been vacated by their owners and repossessed by lenders. A glut of unwanted homes like this has caused upheavals in home sales, and prices have tumbled to rock bottom levels. Although the property values may drop, they always rebound.

Distressed and foreclosed properties are a bargain to buyers. The owners need to unload them quickly for ready cash to pay debts. Many walk out of their homes because they couldn't keep up on the mortgage payments and don't know what else to do. A glut of foreclosed and distressed properties opens the door for opportunity seekers to buy real estate at prices far below their potential value.

Troubled homeowners who are trying to sell their property are doing it out of necessity; they are desperate and want to sell as quickly as possible. Because of this, the asking price will naturally be deflated to assure a quick sale. In any business transaction, if one party is over anxious to make the deal, the other party will benefit the most. The one in a hurry will bend as much as feasible to get rid of the property, even to the extent, in some cases, of taking a tremendous loss.

With the abundance of foreclosed and distressed properties that go on the market and especially during economic recessions, a shrewd buyer can make a killing in real estate. Opportunities exist now and in the near future that have not been available before. And the beauty of it all is that *anybody* can take advantage of the landslide of foreclosures that will hit the market in coming years.

I am not implying that all foreclosed properties are good deals; you have to know where to look for the bargains. Most properties advertised as foreclosures are not bargains. They might be offered for a good price, but you can do better, much better. You will have to search for the real bargains, but they are there, thousands of them, waiting to be picked up for merely a fraction of their value.

There are three ways to buy foreclosed or distressed properties:
(1) during the sale or auction
(2) after the auction
(3) before the auction

In this chapter we will discuss buying property during and after the auction. In Chapter 6 we will cover how to buy the property before the auction.

The first step in buying foreclosed property is locating suitable real estate. You don't go to an auction just hoping to buy a house sight unseen. You must first do your homework. This includes finding a house, personally checking it out, and learning vital facts about it and the sale. You go to the auction fully prepared and knowing the maximum price you are willing to spend on a specific property. This is the only way to buy at foreclosure auctions.

HOW TO FIND PROPERTY IN FORECLOSURE

Where do you look for foreclosed property? There are several places to look. First, let me tell you where not to look for foreclosures. Due to the large inventory of foreclosed homes many lenders, instead of taking a beating by trying to auction them off, have entered the real estate business. Some have even opened up their own real estate offices designed to unload their mounting supply of foreclosed homes. You will see advertisements such as "Foreclosed Homes for Sale" or "For Sale—Foreclosures." These ads are more gimmick than bargain, and the properties sold in this way are usually sold at or near market value. If you're going to buy foreclosed property, you're not interested in fair market value, you want a genuine bargain. Don't even bother to look at any home listed as a foreclosure, it won't be worth your time.

When a lender starts the foreclosure process, he will have a notice posted with the county clerk's office. The county keeps a record of impending foreclosures for public record.

A notice of sale will then be posted on the bulletin board at the courthouse. On the notice will be information, usually incomplete, on where the property is located, the owner, mortgagee, physical description, date and time of sale. Anyone interested in buying these properties can come and look at what is posted. Often, the addresses are missing, and you would then have to search through the courthouse records to find them. If you have the time, you can ask the clerks for help and they will show you what to do.

As an alternative to trying to dig this information up yourself, you can obtain a foreclosure listing. These listings are compiled on a regular bases by people who do the research. They take the notice of sale, track down all pertinent information, and print it up in newsletters or foreclosure listings. These listings are usually sold on a subscription basis, coming out every week or so. This cuts out the hours you may spend in doing the research yourself and gives a complete listing of all properties listed at the courthouse. If you're interested in obtaining a subscription to one of these lists, look on the bulletin board where the notices of sale are posted. Listing companies will often have some type of advertisement there so that interested parties can contact them.

Legal proceedings are often printed in newspapers as a requirement for public notice. This information may be printed in your local newspaper or a legal newspaper.

Announcements are found in the classified ad section under the heading "Legal Notices." In this section you will find notification of foreclosure auctions, estate auctions, and bankruptcy auctions as well as such things as name changes and adoptions.

The information provided usually includes the address, legal description, amount of the current mortgage balance, name of the property owner, lender's

ADDRESS	CURRENT OWNER	LL/D/Z	VAL/YR BLT	MTG INFO	MORTGAGEE	DB/Pg#	ATTORNEY
9549 High St Houston, TX 77033	Young, Beverly	134/15 R	60,990-4/88 1983	44,550 FHA/88/11.5	Owner Gulf Mortgage	3847 456	Joseph Briggs 987-3421
6890 Bay Drive Houston, TX 77033	Stevens, Bob & Lois	78/16 R	65,600-10/85 1985	15,000 2nd/85	Owner First Federal Savings	3374 234	Michael J Foster 440-8543
32409 Hollyhock Houston, TX 77033	Wayne, John & Janice	68/18 R	56,200-TV 1969	22,300 FHA/75/9	Owner First Federal Savings	1422 755	W.R Hennings 809-7744
90080 Gulf Ave. Houston, TX 77033	Blackard, Jeffrey & Carolyn	70/16 R	49,900-TV 1952	21,500 FHA/73/9	Owner Southern Mortgage	2850 122	W.R. Hennings 809-7744
5599 Wellington Terrace Houston, TX 77033	Brunet, James & Christi	151/15 R	87,000-5/88 1987	79,000 FHA/88/10.5	Owner Security Pacific	4990 342	W.R. Hennings 809-7744
9987 Thomas Dr. Houston, TX 77033	Schulz, Dan	188/15 R	74,300-8/85 1984	56,900 ARM/85/7.5	Owner Highland Bank	6594 793	Karyn Ragsdale 607-9581
10603 Cook Rd. Houston, Tx 77033	McKinley, Arthur & LaVern	155/15 R	89,500-TV 1963	39,500 2nd/89	Owner First Federal Savings	2938 493	John Herbert 987-0098
8573 Huntington Venture Houston, TX77045	Hicks, Eric & Jon	12/16 R	66,900-TV 1955	35,000 2nd/86	Owner United Savings & Loan	4090 283	W.R. Hennings 809-7744
50938 Bellaire Ave Houston, TX 77045	Riddle, Adam & Dianne	130/15 R	105,200-TV 1973	87,000 ARM/86/9	Owner United Savings & Loan	3394 203	Joseph Briggs 987-3421
802 Ranch Drive Houston, TX 77045	Dennis, Ray & Dolly	158/15 R	106, 990-8/85 1971	83,000 Cnv/85	Owner Commercial Bank	3450 708	Melvin H Rogers 607-8444
1621 Westpack Houston, TX 77045	Smart, Scott	119/15 R	55,900-TV 1965	40,400 FHA/82	Owner Shaw Financial	4930 483	Melvin H Rogers 607-8444
199 Becket Drive Houston, TX 77043	Webber, Peggy	207/15 R	112,000-11/88 1986	89,500 Cnv/88	Owner Alliance Credit Corp	3928 478	Blaine Shepherd 987-9002
9827 Brburn Bend Sugarland, TX 77042	Hefty, Guy & Margaret	327/18 R	125,900 3/90 1991	92,900 FHA/90/11.5	Owner American Mortgage	5463 596	Frank Sheller 607-9434
882 Holly Drive Sugarland, TX 77042	Roberts, James & Vickie	234/15 R	77,500-TV 1987	57,000 FHA/89/12	Owner FNMA	3092 498	Blake Roberts 607-3827

Sample foreclosure report.

name and the attorney who is handling the foreclosure for the lender. (See sample on preceeding page.) Sometimes only a legal description of the location of the property is given rather than the street address. If the information given is incomplete, you can call the trustee or lawyer and ask for the street address.

The other place to find foreclosures is the legal record for your city. Legal newspapers list all court actions in the area. Most cities over 50,000 or so have these publications. These papers include all legal proceedings occurring in the county and are usually published daily. In smaller cities they might be published once or twice a week. These papers include every bankruptcy, every business license, every bid for government job, every divorce and marriage, all legal notices filed against people and their properties. These are your main avenue to finding properties that have reached the final and serious stage of foreclosure. You can find these at the library or ask an attorney how to get hold of one. Contact the publisher and get on his mailing list.

BUYING AT FORECLOSURE AUCTIONS

The usual method of obtaining foreclosed property is at a foreclosure auction. Before you go to the auction, however, you must be prepared. Not all property offered for sale at a foreclosure auction will be a good deal. Some property will be overpriced and some will be undesirable. You must do the work to figure this out and make a decision if the property holds enough potential for you to spend time and money on. These steps are described below.

Check It Out

Once you have the address and know when and where the sale will take place, go out and examine the property. Don't blindly go to an auction and try to bid on property sight unseen. People have been known to buy property for a drastically low price only to find that it has been extensively damaged by fire or vandalism. Check out the property and the neighborhood. In most cases you will not be able to go inside the house so you will need to peer inside the windows to get an idea of the number and size of rooms. Check the yard thoroughly. Is the house run down, damaged, or termite infested? Is there a sewage treatment plant next door? What is the neighborhood like? Are other homes nearby well kept? Would you like to live in the house yourself? Ask these questions.

Talk to the neighbors. You can learn a lot about a house and the neighborhood by talking to the people who live there. I found one property that looked promising, but when I talked to the neighbors they told me whenever there was a heavy rain the property would flood. I went back to the property,

looked in the crawl space under the house and sure enough I could see that this house was trouble waiting to happen. Signs of water damage was clearly evident under the home. Anyone who bought that home was going to inherit some unwanted headaches. I passed on this one.

Most foreclosed homes are in need of yard work and perhaps some minor repair. It's surprising what a little cosmetic surgery can do to improve the appearance and value of a home. Look at what's needed to get the home in a condition to sell to someone who wants to live there. If the home to trashed out and will require extensive work, it may be best to pass it up. If the price is low enough and their is a healthy amount of equity in the property it may be worth your time to pursue it.

Value the Property

Once you've examined the house and neighborhood, you need to decide the maximum amount you would be willing to pay for it. Before you can do this you need to know the market value of the property. Talk to a real estate agent and see what similar homes in the same neighborhood have sold for. This figure will help you determine the value of the home and give you a yardstick for setting the maximum you will be willing to bid.

It is important that you get as accurate an estimate of the value of the home as possible. The best estimate is to find how much a home with the same floor plan sold for. Also, find out the price of comparables—homes of similar size and amenities. Look for other homes in the area that are for sale and call the Realtors listed on the signs.

Once you know the approximate market value of the home you can determine the equity by subtracting the cost to obtain ownership. Your cost will include the amount of the loan and any fees or penalties you may be required to pay. The difference between what you must pay and the market value is the equity.

How much do you want to earn on the sale of the property? Is $5,000 enough for all your time and effort? Many investors will not even consider a home unless they can make $10,000 - $15,000. That's a good rule to follow because if you allow that much equity, then you have a safe cushion in case of unforeseen circumstances. If the home is slow to sell you may need to lower the price to sell it quickly. You wouldn't be able to lower the price much if you only had $5,000 equity. Plus, you need to consider expenses in fixing up the property, mortgage payments for two or three months while it's on the market, and a little to spare for unforeseen expenses. I would recommend you don't bother with a property unless you can get at least $10,000 in equity. This much equity is not rare, in fact, it's very common. It's not unusual to find homes with $20,000 or more in equity.

You can find the amount needed to pay off back payments and fees and the balance on the loan (the amount the lender needs to satisfy or *cure* the debt) either from the listing or call the lawyer or auction company conducting the sale for that information.

Let's look at an example. Say you set the minimum amount of equity you are looking for after you purchase a property is $10,000. Now, assume that the loan company needs $58,000 to satisfy the loan and another $2,000 to pay off back payments and penalties for a total of $60,000 (this is often the starting bid). You determine that the current market value for the property in question is $85,000. This gives you $15,000 equity. Since your limit is $10,000 in equity, you have $5,000 in which to bargain. In other words, you would be willing to offer as much as $65,000 for the property at auction. This is your limit.

Market value	$85,000
Starting bid	-$60,000
Total Equity	$15,000

Total Equity	$15,000
Minimum equity you require	-$10,000
Amount you have to bargain	$ 5,000

Amount you have to bargain	$ 5,000
Starting bid	+$60,000
The maximum amount you can bid and still retain $10,000 in equity.	$65,000

Setting a minimum limit of $10,000 also allows you some leeway if you overestimate the market value of the property or if you don't sell it a that price (you might give the buyer a discount to get a quick sale).

In this example, if you bid $61,000 and there are no other bidders, that's the amount you pay. And you get the property with $14,000 equity. If someone bids $65,000 or more, you've reached your limit, stop bidding.

Before the Auction

I suggest you go to a few auctions in your area before attempting to buy property and see how the process works. Become familiar with it. The rules will vary from one auction to another. For example, an auction conducted at a sheriff's sale will be handled slightly different than those by the IRS.

Call the auctioneer or trustee and find out the rules and terms of the auction. Their name and phone number will usually be included in the foreclosure listing. At the auction, the rules and terms of the auction are often posted. Ask questions of participants and auctioneers and learn all you need to become an active participant.

The more you know about the auction process the better prepared you will be. Often, there are only a handful of prospective buyers. If there have been a lot of foreclosures and the media has publicized the deals that can be made from foreclosure auctions you may have several dozen people present, mostly curiosity seekers.

When there are a lot of homes to auction, the time posted for the sale will say from 10 AM to 4 PM and that's it. You have no idea when the bidding on your prospect will actually take place. During the auction many trustees will come, auction what property they have, and leave. Several different auctioneers could be auctioning properties at the same time. If you don't know what's happening, the process can be very confusing.

For most people, attending an auction like this is discouraging and cuts their hopes of getting in on the foreclosure market. They may resort to the advertised foreclosures by real estate agents and lending institutions as an alternative. Unless you can pin down the exact time and know who will be auctioning off the property in question, these sales are a waste of time. You don't want to bid on any property sight unseen.

What do you do then? How can you find the right auctioneer and pinpoint the exact time? Is it possible? Yes it is. You will first have to find out, a few days before the auction date, who the auctioneer will be. If the home had been secured with a deed of trust, you would need to contact the trustee and find out from him what time he's going to auction the property. Call up the lender and ask him who the trustee is. The name of the lender is often provided on the notice of sale posted at the courthouse.

Generally, homes are auctioned one at a time. In some cases, a group of homes will be auctioned as a package. Some of the best deals are obtained in this way. A group of eight or ten homes each appraised for around $75,000 could easily sell for an average price of $50,000. The investor who buys them then turns around and sells them each for a $20,000 profit to a buyer who gets them at $5,000 below market value and claims he got the deal of a lifetime. He may even be told he is purchasing foreclosed property and better buy quick because the price is so low investors are clamoring to pick up the good deal. This type of operation can net the investor substantial gains, but obviously not everyone has the financial resources to buy eight homes in one swoop, no matter how good the deal is.

Investor Financing

At this point you may be saying, "I'm ready to cash in on the foreclosure market, but how am I going to get the money to buy the property?"

When you go to the auction you will be expected to put at least 10 percent down on any bid you win. Within about 30 days the balance is due. If you buy a property for $100,000 you will need to bring $10,000 in the form of a cashier's check with you to the auction and pay the remaining $90,000 within a matter of weeks. This thought alone turns most prospective investors and curiosity seekers away from the foreclosure market.

You don't need to have $100,000 in cash lying around to get into the foreclosure market. If you can qualify to borrow the money from the bank, like you would with your own home, you can go that route. All you need is a few thousand dollars for the down payment. You borrow the rest, like you would any mortgage loan. Since your goal will be to turn around and resell the property quickly, you will not be burdened with a loan obligation. You will be free to buy another property and take out a new loan. You do this over and over while only using a few thousand dollars in cash. With each sale you get all of your investment back plus a substantial profit. The profit is substantial because in a matter of weeks you will earn two or three times the amount actually invested.

If you own a home, another option available to you is to use the home as collateral to get a second mortgage. This can supply you with $30,000, $40,000 or more to use for your investment capital. Banks are falling over each other trying to get homeowners to take out equity loans. I receive a couple of pitches in the mail each week from finance companies offering low rates to consolidate credit card and other debts into a home equity loan. These loans are really second mortgages that come with an open line of credit.

With this amount of money you can get started in the foreclosure investment business. At first, you may have to focus on lower priced homes. But as your experience and profits increase you can buy and sell more expensive homes.

At some auctions you won't need to have anywhere near this amount of money because you will assume the original loan. In this case, all you need is enough to pay off back payments and fees. Bidding on such properties (discussed in the next chapter on tax sales) may start out at only one or two thousand dollars with the winning bid well under $10,000. Many times the winning bid may be only a few thousand. You pay the clerk at the auction and assume the existing loan. If you resell the home quickly you avoid having to make any mortgage payments. Once you've earned enough to pay back your second mortgage you may decide to do that or you may keep the cash and continue using it. Taking out a home equity loan to get the capital you need isn't necessarily the best way to go, but it is an option if you can't find financing any other way.

Why risk your own money if you don't have to? You can buy foreclosed property without investing any of your own money. The way you do this is by using leverage, that is, other people's money.

Let's say you find an investor who loans you the money you need. You buy and sell a property and net a $10,000 profit after paying back the loan. What does your lender receive? You will have to cut him in on the profit to make it worth his risk. If you split the money 50/50 you each bring home $5,000. You risk no money of your own and reap a $5,000 gain. Even if you only earn $2,000 - $3,000 would it be worth your time? That's all it cost you—time.

You might be thinking, "Why would anyone give me money to invest in real estate? If they have the money, couldn't they just do it themselves?" Who are the people with the money to invest?—doctors, dentists, and business owners—people who are busy running their own businesses. They don't have the time or the know-how to invest in the foreclosure market, but they do have the money. Keep in mind, that you are the foreclosure expert. You know how to find and evaluate profitable properties and you can make them a lot of money. If you do all the research and the leg work, don't you think it's worth it to an investor to split the profits with you? You bet it is.

You don't need a lot of money to cash in on the foreclosure market. What you need is *access* to the money. It doesn't have to be your money. Why risk your money when you can use other people's money. That's the key. Find someone who does have the money. They put up the money while you contribute your expertise, time, and effort. Your profits can be split with the investor at 50/50, 45/55 or however you decide.

Where do you find investors? You can find them by advertising. Place an ad in the real estate or business opportunities classified ad section of the newspaper. You can state something like, "I will locate foreclosures if you will finance" or "Real estate investor looking for partner". You will get many calls. Explain what you are able to do for them. Let them know, that you are an expert (regardless of how many properties you've actually dealt with) and will make them a lot of money. Let them know the potential, that you will be able to buy properties at 20, 30 and even 40 percent below market value. You will make several thousand dollars each time you resell the property. Show them that you know what you're doing. Most investors will be professionals and although they know about their own profession, they will know very little about real estate investment, and even less about foreclosures. This is your specialty.

If you can buy property at 20, 30, and 40 percent below market value, investors will be interested. You can show them how they can make $10,000 in just a few weeks and they don't have to do anything but invest the money.

In time, when word gets out about how much you make on each transaction, investors will start seeking you out. You won't have any trouble finding the money to finance your investments.

When you go to the auction you need to bring funds with you. The investor can make out a check to you that you can endorse over to the trustee. Or you may bring the investor with you to the auction. This way he can write out check for the deposit himself. While you may bring your investor with you, do not teach him too much of what you do or he may become a competitor if he has the time. Most investors are busy people and are more than willing to give you money and leave the leg work up to you. They have busy careers which don't allow them time to spend learning about the foreclosure market and doing everything that is necessary in the process.

At the Auction

After you have determined the maximum amount you can bid, you have financing available, and you know what terms and conditions to expect in order to acquire the property, then you are ready for the auction.

The auction may be held on the property, in which case you will have the opportunity to examine the inside of the house. The auction may also take place at the courthouse or the auctioneer's office.

On the day of the auction you may need to register, show a cashier's check made out to yourself (to be endorsed over to the auction company if you are the successful bidder), and obtain a bidder card and number.

By far the most common type of bidding is where the auctioneer starts the bidding at a certain price and then takes bids. Potential buyers bid against each other with the highest bidder getting the property.

Another type of bidding which you may come across is the sealed bid. In this case, potential buyers write down how much they are willing to pay and enclose it in a sealed envelope. Bidders make only one bid each. They usually bid the maximum amount they are willing to pay for the property. All bids are opened and the highest bid wins.

Whether its an open or sealed bid, the seller isn't obligated to accept the highest bid if he considers it too low. But most high offers are usually accepted. The main reason a seller may not accept a bid is because it will not allow the seller to recoup expenses. Most sellers are primarily interested in unloading the property without suffering a loss and are not out to make a profit. So they will accept any offer as long as it pays their expenses.

At the start of the auction, the auctioneer will state the terms of the auction and describe each property about to be auctioned. He will begin with a legal description of the property, state the amount of the loan, the mortgage balance, the interest that is due and owing, and the amount of the court costs and foreclosure costs up to that point. He will lump them together in one sum and then state the total that the trustee or mortgagee bids.

The amount the lender will bid will usually equal what is owed on the loan. He does this so that the property does not sell for less than the outstanding loan amount. If someone bids higher, the lender gets his money back.

The auctioneer will ask for any other bids, and if there is nobody there or nobody makes a bid he will say, "Going once, going twice, trustee takes possession, gone." The lender assumes ownership of the property. If he gets the property back he will try to sell it at another auction or list it with a real estate broker. If it is listed with a Realtor the lender must pay a commission and expenses for keeping the house in decent condition for resell. So, the price will be much higher than the lender's original bid price at auction. These are the ones you will see advertised in the newspapers as foreclosed homes.

There are basically two reasons why a property will not sell at a foreclosure auction. The first is because no buyers showed up at the auction or those buyers who did attend showed no interest in the property. Usually, there are only a few people that go to these auctions. At times, you may be the only one there. The second reason a house won't sell is because even at the opening bid it is overpriced. If the opening bid for a property is at or near the market value most investors will not touch it. More than likely the property will need some clean up or repairs which will take time and money and it's just not worth it. If a buyer has to pay full market price he might as well go though a Realtor and get a home that has been well taken care of and won't need extra work. Of course, the only ones who would want this type of property are those looking for a home to live in themselves not for an investment.

At the auction you will only be interested in the property you have researched and are prepared to bid on. It may be the only home offered at the auction that day or it may be one of several. Once the opening bid has been announced you can make a higher bid. Bid as low as you can but never go over the limit you have set. If someone else bids higher, let them have it; other properties are available. Don't get emotionally involved or caught up in a bidding war. Keep in control. This is a business operation and if the price gets too high, let it go.

If you make the winning bid, you will most likely be required to make a cash deposit of 10 percent of the purchase price at the time of sale. The balance of the bid would become due at closing a month or so later. The amount of the deposit and the time the balance is due varies from state to state so you will need to ask your lawyer or the auctioneer about this before the auction. In some states the entire amount is required at the time of sale.

After the Sale

After you have paid your down payment, you essentially become the owner. Although officially you won't assume ownership until closing. Closing may be a month away, but don't wait until then to start selling the house. Start immediately. Prepare your newspaper ads and listing sheet (this is explained in detail in Chapter 8). Evaluate all work that needs to be done and schedule someone to do it. Start as much as you can before your closing takes place. If you do this you will resell the property before you have to make a single mortgage payment. Many investors have commitments from buyers before they even reach closing.

In Chapter 8 I will show you how to market and sell your property in the shortest amount of time possible. You will learn how to sell homes and make a profit even in a buyers' market when real estate isn't selling well.

The process of finding properties, checking them out, buying them, and reselling takes time. You can do it as a part-time means of earning extra income. Many do it full-time. But you do have to devote time, effort, and money. The only way you will be able to make a decent profit in this process is if you carefully select the homes you buy. Go after only those that have the potential of bringing you at least $10,000 or more after all expenses are paid. To do this you must deal with property which has at least $10,000-$15,000 in equity. Don't waste time with anything less, unless all you plan to do with the property is rent it out and wait for it to appreciate in value. Renting is a slower way to make money, but many investors do it.

Redemption Period

One thing you need to be aware of when buying property at a foreclosure sale is the redemption period. The redemption period is the time the former homeowner has to make up back payments and penalties to redeem or reclaim ownership the property. The period allowed varies from state to state (see chart on page 26). It can be as little as 10 days or less to as long as a year or more. Some states don't even have a redemption period.

It is important for you to know the redemption period in your state. If you live in an area that allows a year for the former homeowner to reclaim property you've purchased, that means you may not resell it until then. You would have to hold on to the property for a full year. Obviously, in this case you would have to turn it into a income producing property by renting it out in order to keep from losing money. There is nothing wrong with this, but you don't normally make money by renting, you make money by selling. Your profit in the home will be delayed for a year. You must decide if it's worth it to you.

If you buy a property in an area that allows a redemption and the former owner claims property, what happens? You may not be able to sell the property until the redemption period is over. If the former owner can pay off all debt he owes on property then it will be given back to him. Obviously, you have spent a lot of time and money acquiring the property. You should be compensated. And you are. You're paid a rate of interest on your money you paid for the property. This is usually paid at the end of the redemption period in a lump sum. The interest rate is usually quit high 20% or so, and in some areas as much as 50% or more. So, even if you don't keep the property you can receive an substantial profit if it is redeemed.

BUYING FORECLOSURES AFTER THE AUCTION

I've explained how to buy foreclosures during the auction, now let me explain how you can get foreclosures after the auction. While the normal way to buy foreclosed property is during the foreclosure auction, you can also pick up some tremendous deals after the auction.

At most auctions there is usually only a handful of people. At times you may be the only one present. Sometimes you will encounter 20 or 30 people if a lot of property is being auctioned off, but generally attendance is sparse.

It is not uncommon for properties to go unsold at auctions. This means the bank is stuck with the property. This is not a good thing. Banks aren't in the real estate business and they don't want the property. This property is known as real estate owned (REO) and represents defaulted loans which looks bad on their records. Federal regulations dictate how long the lender has to sell the property and remove these assets from its books. And their records are continually being audited by state and federal authorities. So they are anxious to get rid of this property as quickly as possible.

They've already tired unloading the property at a foreclosure auction and that didn't work. Now they're stuck with it.

These properties must be sold and the lender's books cleaned up. Usually they're dumped on the market and sold through real estate agents like any other property. Sometimes, in order to stimulate sales the bank will advertise them as foreclosures. People see the word "foreclosure" and think they will get a bargain. But the homes sold this way aren't necessarily bargains. The buyer will be paying close to full market value for the property at this stage.

Usually, the property needs fixing up to make it presentable and entice prospective buyers. So the lender must spend money to fix it up. Since the bank has to pay money to on upkeep and a Realtor's commission when it sales, the price of the home must be increased to avoid losing money.

Banks are anxious to get rid of the REO property and are willing to sell at bargain prices just to get them off their books. You can ask a Realtor if he has any REOs available. If he does and you find some worth pursuing, you might make an offer, but make it at least 15 percent or more below the list price. If the bank is eager to sell, they may accept the offer or come back with a counter offer. Keep in mind as you negotiate, that you need to buy the property at a price that will allow you to quickly resell and make a profit.

Although you may get some good deals working through a Realtor, if you bypass the agent and deal with the bank directly you will save them the expense of a commission and will likely get the property much cheaper. But, you can't just go into the bank and ask to buy their REOs. That won't work. REOs represent bad loans and they don't want people to think their bank is burdened with unpaid debts.

So, you need to use some tact. First thing you need to do is get business cards printed with your name and address stating "Real Estate Investor", or "I Buy Real Estate" or something to that effect. A business card is important because it lets others know you are a professional and you know what you are doing. It's a sign of legitimacy, and its cheap. Hand these cards out to every one you meet. You will get calls that will land you some great deals.

With business cards ready, call up the bank and ask to speak with one of the vice presidents, preferably one who handles real estate loans or REOs. Don't talk with the branch manager or anyone else because you need someone with authority who can make a deal with you. Make an appointment to come in and talk for a few minutes. You don't need to explain much over the phone. You need an appointment. Don't just stop by and expect to see them, as they are busy and won't want to deal with you. Make sure you meet the banker face to face. You want to establish a working relationship with this person and a faceless voice over the phone won't do it.

Give the vice president your card and explain that you are an investor and are looking for properties to invest in. Express an interest in any REOs they might have.

They will probably say, "we don't have any" or "we usually don't have many of those." They don't know you and they're not likely to say, "why yes, we've got 10 or 12 bad loans to get rid of." Your goal in this first meeting is simply to hand out your business card and let him know you're looking for these type of properties. Don't waste a lot of time.

You can visit several different banks, savings and loans, and credit unions. Not all will be fruitful. Eventually it will payoff. Some will give you a call and they will say, "weren't you looking to buy some property awhile back? Well, we may have something you might be interested in."

What they will probably try to do is have you give them a down payment and take over the existing loan or take out a new loan at a high rate of interest. Don't deal with them on those terms. Each of these properties represents a bad business decision on their part and they want to get rid of them. You want to get the best possible deal you can. You are in a position to bargain and they can and will make all kinds of concessions to unload the property.

They can do any number of things to make the property more appealing to you. For example, they can lower the price, lower the interest rate a couple of points, or allow you to make no payments for 6 or 8 months or more. They are at liberty to do all sorts of things if you approach them right. All you have to do is negotiate. You might tell them you will pay the price they're asking if you can lower the interest rate or hold off on payments for a few months. Not making payment for several months is a good strategy because it gives you time to resell the property without making monthly payments. They don't really lose anything because having the property sit in their possession isn't giving them any monthly income either, but they are getting rid of the property.

All terms are negotiable. You'll find out who is willing to work with you and who isn't. Don't waste time with those who won't negotiate. Keep in mind you're helping them as much, or more, than they are helping you.

In areas of the country the get cold at winter time you have an advantage. If you approach the banks in the fall, you will have more success. You may even get more responses than you can possible handle. Why? Because they have to pay for maintenance and during the winter that includes heating. Without heat, water pipes may burst. Vandalism is always a problem with vacant houses. So banks are especially anxious to dump the property before winter hits. Bankers are used to negotiating so don't expect them to offer you very favorable terms at first. Remember, they don't want these properties and if they don't sell to you, they will be stuck with them. There are many other properties available, so negotiate terms that will be most favorable to you.

Some lenders have REO departments for properties that they have taken back through foreclosure. You can contact the banks, savings and loans, and credit and finance companies and ask if they have an REO department. DataSource RE, Inc. is a company that provides a monthly newsletter about REO properties as well as a list of lender contacts and the properties they currently have in their portfolios. For more information contact DataSource RE, Inc., 736 Seventh St., Boulder, CO 80302. 800-477-9194.

5

REAL AND PERSONAL PROPERTY

In the last chapter you learned how to buy property from banks and other lenders. There are also other types of foreclosure auctions available that can provide excellent opportunities to get property at rock bottom prices—far below market value.

In the previous chapter you learned that in order to buy property at a foreclosure auction you must have a sizable chunk of money readily available or be able to quality for a home loan. But what about the person who doesn't have much money and can't qualify for loan on a second home, or can't find an investor to join him, can he still get into the foreclosure market? Yes! This chapter will explain how.

NON-LENDER FORECLOSURES

Banks and finance companies aren't the only ones who repossess property and have it sold at auctions. The government, both local and federal, confiscates property all the time to satisfy delinquent taxes or other debts. In this book I distinguish these from the ones described in the previous chapter by calling them *non-lender foreclosures*. These properties aren't foreclosed on because of failure to pay the lender, they're taken for not paying some other type of debt. These auctions are much less publicized and virtually unknown to the general public. Here you can get some excellent bargains without using a lot of cash.

Since these properties were seized to pay delinquent debts, they are sold for the amount owed, which could be as little as $1,000 or less! The federal or local government will not hesitate to foreclose on someone's house to satisfy a delinquent tax debt, even if the debt is only a couple of hundred dollars! These homes will be put up for sale to pay the debt. Their only concern is to get enough to satisfy the debt, not sell the property at market value or make a profit. Consequently, these homes sell for amounts far below what they are worth. Could you imagine yourself acquiring a three bedroom home for $2,000? You can do it. It's done all the time. I acquired by first house this way for only $3,500. It had a market value of about $45,000.

Where do you go to learn about these properties? There are several government agencies that have the authority to seize property and sell it at a public auction. The biggest is the Department of Housing and Urban Development (HUD). HUD handles foreclosed properties from the Federal Housing Administration (FHA) and the Veterans Administration (VA). The Federal National Mortgage Association (FNMA), affectionately known as Fanny Mae, also conducts auctions. Information on these auctions can be found advertised in the real estate section of your newspaper or by calling your local HUD office.

Other agencies which auction property are the Internal Revenue Service (IRS), the Drug Enforcement Administration (DEA), the Justice Department (U.S. Marshall's office), the City Tax Department, and the County Tax Assessor. Go to their offices, they will have a bulletin board where they will post notices of sales of seized property just as the county courthouse does. These notices are usually more complete than the ones filed at the courthouse. They provide the address of the property, brief description, time and date of sale, and often the minimum bid.

Professional auctioneers usually auction off the property and get paid a percentage of whatever they sell the property for. You can call them up and ask for specific information about the sale. They will be more than happy to give it to you because your participation will add to the competition and increase bids, which will increase their commission.

You can phone them up and tell them you're an investor and would like to have your name put on their mailing list. You will then be notified of upcoming auctions and all particulars. They will do this willingly for real estate investors. If you tell them you are only looking for a single property for a residence, they will give you some information over the phone but will not want to waste time by adding you to their mailing list. The auctioneer knows once you've purchased a residence, if that's all you're interested in, any material he sends you will be discarded. Ask the agency who has posted the notice of sale, who will be auctioning the property, or look up auctioneers in the Yellow Pages.

You can get some excellent bargains this way, but not without some hurdles to overcome. One problem you may face is having the former owner try to reclaim the property. In cases where a house was seized for unpaid taxes, the debtor is allowed a certain amount of time in which he can reclaim it. By paying all back taxes, costs incurred from the foreclosure, and a small commission to the buyer (you), he can get back possession of the home. This time given to the debtor will vary from state to state so you may want to inquire about regulations in your own area. Even though there is a possibility that your bargain will be snatched out of your hands by the former owner, in most cases the property will remain yours.

Another hurdle you must jump is dealing with the lender who has the mortgage. Although you paid for the property, what you actually bought was the equity or the portion of the property that was owned by the former owner. The mortgagee still has a lien on the property and can foreclose on the new owner if payments are not made. In essence, what you have done by purchasing a piece of property at a government sponsored auction is obtain all the ownership the former owner had and assume his loan. You acquire all of the equity in the home, but you also become responsible for paying the mortgage. At first, this may sound like a can of worms, but you can get some excellent bargains this way none-the-less. In the case of many city and county auctions, all other liens become null and void, so you don't have to worry about paying off these lenders.

Let's assume you are interested in some property that still holds the lender's lien. This home may be valued at $90,000 and may have $50,000 left to pay on the mortgage. If you can buy it at auction for $15,000, you will be getting the house for only $65,000. You can then turn around and resell it for its market value giving you a $25,000 profit! If you can sell it soon enough after the sale to avoid paying the monthly mortgage payments, your total investment would have been only the $15,000. You would reap a 167 percent profit!

In preparing for the auctions described in this chapter you must go through basically the same procedures described in Chapter 4. You need to find out when the auction is to take place, visit the property, evaluate the maximum amount you will be willing to invest, and have the financing readily available. Since each auction will have slightly different rules and regulations, you need to find out what they are. You can find this out by calling and talking to the trustee or auctioneer. You also need to go to the auctions before you become a bidder to see how they are conducted.

BANKRUPTCY SALES

Bankruptcies are regulated by federal laws so, procedures are fairly uniform from state to state. The court will appoint a trustee. The trustee's job is to liquidate assets of the debtor to pay creditors. Assets include both personal property and real estate. If the debater doesn't have much equity in his home and wants to keep it, a bankruptcy can prevent him from losing it if he continues to make regular payments. If the homeowner has too much equity in the home, it must be sold to help satisfy his debts.

The trustee is not too concerned about getting full market value on the property being sold. His primary concern is with liquidating all the assets as quickly as possible.

The trustee will hold either a public auction or sealed bid. Keep in mind that the trustee is not obligated to accept highest bid. If bid is extremely low he can refuse it. However, in most cases he will accept just about any bid. If you win the bid you must pay in cash, cashier's check, or money order before leaving the auction.

In order to find out when sales occur, you will want to get on the mailing list of various bankruptcy courts in your area. This information is usually published in legal newspapers or newspapers of general circulation. Contact the bankruptcy court in your area and ask them to add your name to their mailing list. You can look them up in the White Pages of the phone book under United States or Federal District Court.

ESTATE SALES

Estates sales happen when there has been a death and property has to be sold to satisfy an estate. These sales are usually announced in local newspapers and in legal newspapers.

Usually oral bidding is done at estate sales. You know in advance when the sale is to be. Go look at the property. Contact the trustee or people still living in the home to take a look at it. Then determine the value.

Property sold at estate sales are free of liens. Once you by it that's it, you don't need to worry about back taxes or liens of any sort.

As always, decide how much you are willing to bid. At the auction there probably won't be many people there because most people simply aren't aware of these auctions. How many people do you know who subscribes to legal newspaper? Not many, most don't know what it is. This is an excellent opportunity to pickup real estate as well as other merchandise.

IRS SALES

Although most of us dislike the IRS, it does provide excellent opportunity for investors to buy real estate at rock bottom prices.

When taxpayers are delinquent in paying their taxes, the Internal Revenue Service will seize their assets and sell them to pay off or pay down the amount owed.

A notice will appear in the newspaper ten days before the auction. Included with this announcement will be a list of all current encumbrances on the property. The advertising and the actual sale will take place in the county where the property is located, or on the local courthouse steps. All sales are "as is, where is". There is a six-month redemption period in which the taxpayer can redeem the property. If property is redeemed by the taxpayer he must pay the purchaser (you) back the amount you paid plus an additional 20 percent. At times, the redemption period is waived in order to encourage a higher bidding price. The IRS usually conducts the auctions itself, but for some larger properties it may use the services of an outside auction company.

Bidding might be either sealed or oral. Property will go to the highest bidder. Although they are not obligated to sell to the highest bidder, they usually will. They want to get at least as much as is owed to them. They're not too concerned with the market value of the property, they just want to get the amount necessary to satisfy the debt. This can really be crazy as you can pick up homes with tens of thousands of dollars in equity for only a couple of thousand dollars.

You need to know if there are any liens against the property. You need to know this. The IRS will give this information to you if you ask because they want to sell the property. Call them and inquire about liens and encumbrances. All liens are not wiped out when property is sold at an IRS auction, so the buyer becomes responsible. Be careful.

When you talk with the people at the IRS they will give you what they know at the time and it's usually accurate, but to be sure you may want to double check. To find out if there are other mortgages or liens on the property you can use a title company or real estate lawyer to find this information out for you. Once you know this, add the numbers and see if after paying off all liens you will still make enough to make it worth your while. Just because a home does have a lien doesn't mean it isn't a good deal. Your calculations will tell you if there is enough equity in the home to absorb any other liens.

Sometimes the IRS will run notices in the local newspaper. Notices are also posted on the bulletin board in the IRS office. Call IRS office in your area for details. If you call, don't be surprised if you have to talk to three or four different people before you find someone who knows anything about what you're talking about. People working in the IRS office may have little idea what others around them do.

Ask to speak to a supervisor. He can direct you to the right person. Have him put you on their mailing list. Get the IRS agent's name and business address. Write a short note to this person as reminder to "please put my name on your mailing list for upcoming auctions of real and personal property" to jog his memory, as he very well may forget.

LAW ENFORCEMENT AUCTIONS

There are several law enforcement agencies that seize property and sell it at auctions. This property is confiscated for various reasons, ranging from unpaid legal judgments and delinquent taxes to abandonment. Most of this type of property is merchandise, but can also include real estate. Property in this category is seized by the federal, state, county, or city governments.

Property confiscated by the federal government is usually sold through the United States Marshal's Office. Federal agencies include the Federal Bureau of Investigation (FBI), U.S. Customs Office, Drug Enforcement Administration (DEA), and Internal Revenue Service (IRS). Since these are federal agencies the rules and regulations governing the each auction are fairly uniform from state to state.

On a local scale you have sheriffs auctions. Sheriffs sales occur when a person has gone to court and has had a judgment against him and he refuses to pay the judgment. Property is confiscated and sold to satisfy the judgment.

These sales are conducted under the jurisdiction of state courts, so rules vary from state to state. In some states there is no redemption, all sales are final. In other states their may be a redemption period. You need to find out what it is in your area. You do this by calling the sheriffs office or go down and talk to someone at their office.

Notices for the law enforcement sales are posted at the post office, court house, or the agency's office. Sometimes they may be announced in the newspaper. To make sure you are aware of each sale you need to get on their mailing list if they have one. Some places will put you on their list for free, others may charge. Give the law enforcement office a call and ask to be placed on their mailing list or find out how they advertise their auctions.

HUD FORECLOSURES

HUD foreclosures are FHA and VA insured loans that have defaulted. The department of Housing and Urban Development (HUD) takes over the properties and sells them. These types of loans are made by banks and other lenders just as conventional loans are, but they are backed or guaranteed by the federal government. If someone with one of these loans defaults, HUD pays the lender and takes over the property. The property is then put on the market for sale. The procedure for buying this type of property is uniform from state to state because the real estate becomes federal property.

Anyone who meets the down payment, credit and other requirements of the local lender can make an offer to purchase HUD property. HUD offers properties for sale only through local real estate brokers. Brokers earn commissions for HUD sales and are happy to work with anyone interested in buying this type of property.

When HUD takes over a property it is boarded up, the door is locked, and a notice is posted. All HUD owned properties are offered for sale in an "as is" condition. That means they may be run down, or have some serious structural damage. The agency will offer no warranty on any property for sale. Some properties may need extensive repairs to satisfy building codes. So it is important you check them out thoroughly. Most foreclosed homes, whether they are HUD or not will need some maintenance. Not all HUD homes are in need of major repair. See what needs be done to fix it up. Often it is something rather minor that can be corrected without too much expense and may still make a very good investment.

HUD advertises properties for sell in local newspapers. You can contact your local HUD office for a listing of available properties. Real estate brokers will also have a listing.

With HUD homes you can use a Realtor to help. HUD will pay the Realtor's commission for each sale. It doesn't cost you anything and they can help. They have a key to the lock on the door and can show you around the property. They will be happy to do so because if you buy it, they will earn a commission. This is one of the few times you will be able to go inside and examine the home before you make an offer.

HUD accepts bids up to a specified date, usually set at ten days from the date property is listed. Bids must be accompanied by a earnest money deposit that varies from $500 to $2,000. The amount is established by each local HUD office.

Each HUD home has a listed asking price. Keep in mind, this is the *asking* price and not necessarily the price the home will sell at. They will usually accept less.

HUD is primarily interested in unloading the property as quickly as possible and recoup as much of the money they spent on it as they can. The property will be listed close to market value. You, however, don't pay market value on property—at least not after reading this book.

If the home is listed for $80,000, do your homework and see how much you would be willing to pay for it and still be able to make a profit when you resell. You may have the real estate agent submit an offer of $60,000. This may sound extremely low, for a property which may very well be worth $85,000 to $90,000 especially after it has been spruced up a bit with a little yard work and cleanup. But you never know, it may be accepted. Why offer $75,000 when you can get it for $60,000?

I recommend that you make an offer that is 80 percent of the asking price. If the list price is $80,000 then 80 percent would be $64,000. That's what you offer. Most offers of this type will be rejected, but so what, go for those that will sell for less than market value. Perhaps one out of ten. You don't have anything to lose.

In order to bid on a HUD owned property, the purchaser must complete a HUD sales contract (HUD Form 9548). The contract must be signed by the purchaser and the real estate broker. The bid is submitted by the broker. All bids are rounded to the nearest dollar amount. Each bid is submitted in a sealed envelope.

If property is not sold during the initial listing period, it is relisted, perhaps with a different price or other terms. Sometimes property will stay on the market for months. If you track these and find one that has been around for awhile, you know it will probably be sold at considerably below its list price.

Accepted bids are acknowledged by mail or by telephone through the real estate broker who submitted the bid. Rejected bids are returned by mail. If the bid is rejected, your earnest money deposit is returned to you by the real estate broker.

If the winning bid failed to close for some reason, some HUD offices will accept the next highest bid in its place. Closing takes place within the time specified by the local HUD office, usually 30 to 60 days. Your local HUD office can provide you will full details on what's available in your area and procedure requirements. HUD offices are listed in Appendix B.

FHA and VA property sold through HUD are handled about the same. The only major difference is that VA property is almost always sold at full list price. So don't waste time making an offer less than that. Only when they advertise that below-list offers will be considered can you try with any hope of success.

Besides single family dwellings HUD also has muli-family properties like duplexes and apartments. These are not for the beginner because of the expense involved in purchasing this type of property. But if you're interested or have reached this stage, you can contact your local HUD office for a list of such properties.

FANNIE MAE AND FREDDIE MAC PROPERTIES

There are two other entities similar to HUD whereby you can acquire property. The Federal National Mortgage Association (FNMA), or Fannie Mae as it is commonly known, is a private corporation owned by over 35,000 shareholders. The other is the Federal Home Loan Mortgage Corporation (FHLMC), commonly known as Freddie Mac, and was originally established to provide a secondary mortgage market for the nation's savings and loan associations. It provides low-cost mortgage funds to individuals with moderate incomes. Fannie Mae properties are sold either through local real estate brokers or by auction. Freddie Mac properties are available only through real estate brokers. Some properties may be fixed up while others are sold "as is".

Fannie Mae and Freddie Mac are willing to negotiate the property's price, the earnest-money deposit, and the closing costs. They can also provide financing at market rates.

To obtain a listing of properties that are currently available contact FNMA Foreclosures, P.O. Box 13165, Baltimore, MD 21203, 800-553-4636. A list of both FNMA and FHLMC offices can be found in Appendix B.

THE SMALL BUSINESS ADMINISTRATION

The Small Business Administration (SBA) is a government agency that makes loans to small businesses. These loans are primarily to finance the purchase of furniture, equipment, and inventory, but also includes real estate.

When a loan is defaulted, property which is used as collateral is confiscated by SBA and sold either though public auction or sealed bid.

DISTRICT COURT, COUNTY OF EL PASO STATE OF COLORADO Case No. 97CV2377 Division 3
SHERIFF'S NOTICE OF SALE
PCG-ORLANDO LLC, a Colorado limited liability company,
Plaintiff,
vs.
JAMES BERRY CRADDOCK, doing business as CRADDOCK DEVELOPMENT COMPANY; CRADDOCK DEVELOPMENT COMPANY, INC., a Colorado corporation; and ESTHER E. RINARD, in her capacity as Public Trustee of El Paso County,
Defendants.
Under a Findings and Decree of Foreclosure entered July 22, 1998, in the above action, I am ordered to sell the following property, which is all of the property currently encumbered by the Deed of Trust described in said Findings and Decree of Foreclosure.
The north ½ of Lot 1, Block 1, Rustic Hills North Filing No. 4-A, as recorded in Plat Book J-3 at Page 44 of the records of El Paso County, Colorado.
and
The west ½ of Lot 3, Block 1, Rustic Hills North Filing No. 4-1, as recorded in Plat Book J-3 at Page 44 of the records of El Paso County, Colorado
The plaintiff named above is the judgment creditor in this action and the current owner of the evidence of debt (the judgment entered herein) secured by the property being sold: as of June 30, 1998, the outstanding balance due and owing on such judgment is $70,000.
I shall offer for public sale to the highest bidder, for cash, at public auction, all the right, title and interest of the defendant in said property on December 3, 1998, at 10:00 o'clock a.m. at the El Paso County Sheriff's Office, 205 South Cascade Avenue, Colorado Springs, Colorado.
DATED this 28th day of September, 1998.
JOHN WESLEY ANDERSON, Sheriff, El Paso County, Colorado By: /s/ Sgt. B.J. Mattson

Department of the Treasury/Internal Revenue Service
Notice of
Sealed Bid Sale
Under the authority in Internal Revenue Code section 6331, the property described below has been seized for nonpayment of internal revenue taxes due from John & Sarah Smith, 4435 Spring Rd, Auburn, CA 95825

The property will be sold at public sale under sealed bid as provided by Internal Revenue Code section 6335 and related regulations.

Date Bids will be Opened: March 28, 1999.

Time Bids will be Opened: 10:00 a.m.

Place of Sale: 55 Hilton Ave, Auburn, CA 95825, Room 16.

Title Offered: Only the right, title and interest of John and Sarah Smith in and to the property will be offered for sale. If requested, the Internal Revenue Service will furnish information about possible encumbrances, which may be useful in determining the value of the interest being sold.

Submission of Bids: All bids must be submitted on Form 2222, Sealed Bid for Purchase of Seized Property. Contact the office indicated below for Forms 2222 and information about the property. Submit bids to the person named below before the time bids will be opened.

Payment terms: Bids must be accompanied by the full amount of the bid if it totals $200 or less. If the total bid is more than $200, submit 20 percent of the amount of bid.

Form of Payment: All payments must be cash, certified check, cashier's check or by a United States postal bank, express or telegraph money order. Make check or money order payable to the Internal Revenue Service.

R. Johnson
Revenue Officer
55 Hilton Ave, Auburn, CA 95825, Room 16.

Sample of various notices of foreclosure sales.

FANNIE MAE
AUCTION

7.5%
FINANCING
Selling by order of the Federal National Mortgage Association

SALE SITE: The Inter-Continental Hotel, 5150 Westheimer
THE FOLLOWING PROPERTIES SELL MON., MARCH 23RD AT 7:00 PM

10931 Dunvegan Way Houston, TX 77244 3 BR, 2 bath, 2,103 SF Home	5929 Southgood Houston, TX 77245 2BR, 1 bath, 1,008 SF Home	234 Village Bend Houston, TX 77033 3 BD, 3 bath, 2,260 SF Home	29207 Loddington Spring, TX 77034 3 BR, 2 bath, 1,714 SF Home
8018 Ithaca Houston, TX 77234 2 BR, 1 bath, 1,411 SF Home	16103 Espinosa Houston, TX77245 4 BR 2 bath, 2,297 SF Home	155 Camino Del Sol Houston, TX 77033 4 BD, 3 bath, 2,455 SF Home	3322 Burk Road Pasadena, TX 77037 3 BR, 2 bath, 1,512 SF Home
3434 Brookstone Street Houston, TX 77244 4 BR, 2 bath, 2,300 SF Home	17723 Field glen Dr. Houston, TX 77245 2 BR, 2 bath1,400 SF Home	10930 Village Bend #66 Houston, TX 77033 2 BD, 2 bath, SF Townhome	8130 Glenn Lane Pasadena, TX 77037 3 BR, 2 bath, 1,870 SF Home

AUCTION REGISTRATION: Registration and financing pre-qualification will begin at 5:00 PM on day of sale. Please come early to avoid delay. Cashier's check in the amount of $2,000 must be shown at the time of registration

TERMS: Owner-occupants pay 5% of bid price down at the auction and investors pay 10% of bid price down at the auction of which $2,000 must be in cashier's check for each unit purchased. Investors planning to buy multiple properties may bring a $6,000 cashier's check. The remainder of the down payment, if any, may be paid by personal check. Cashier's check should be made payable to yourself. Balance of purchase price due at closing within 1- to 40 days after date of sale. All cash sales are expected to close on or before April 2nd. Specific closing dates to be scheduled at the auction.

FINANCING: For the convenience of the purchasers, Fannie Mae and Hudson and Marshall, Inc. have arranged for three leading lending institutions to be at the auction to provide special financing for qualified purchasers.

IMPORTANT NOTICE
In the event the Buyer does not qualify for the financing provided by Fannie Mae, or chooses not to use Fannie Mae financing, the Buyer must arrange his/her own financing or purchase for cash. If the Buyer cannot purchase the property because he/she is unable to arrange financing or purchase for cash, the Buyer will be in default and will forfeit his/her earnest money. No VA or FHA financing allowed. This is a cash contract.

FINANCING TERMS: 95% financing available to owner-occupants, 30-year fixed at 7.5%. 80% financing available to investors, 30-year fixed 8%.

LOAN CHARGES: If financing is provided by Fannie Mae, Buyer shall pay up to 3% of the sales price for loan and closing charges, including Owner's Title Insurance, Mortgagee's Title Policy, first year's premium for private mortgage insurance (if required), and loan origination fee. Seller shall pay any excess. Normal prepaids and pre-rated items are the responsibility of the Buyer and are in addition to the Buyer's responsibility for loan and closing charges. If financing is not provided by Fannie Mae, the Buyer is required to pay all normal and customary loan and closing charges, including Owner's Title Insurance. Fannie Mae shall only be responsible for the following costs: 1) Commission Fee, 2) Tax Certificate, and 3) Deed Preparation.

PRE-QUALIFYING: For your convenience we have financing guideline approval forms available. Call the Auctioneers to receive your forms at no obligation.

BROKER PARTICIPATION: Brokers wishing to register prospective clients for this auction must contact Randy Smiley in Houston (713) 787-4112 by Monday, March 16th at 5:00 PM

Hudson and Marshall, Inc
Realtor and Auctioneers
717 North Avenue
Macon, Georgia 31211
(912)743-1511

The vast majority of property sold by the SBA is through public auction. A Local auction company is used and will advertise the property in the newspaper. The highest bidder must deposit between 10-25 percent of the bid price and then close within the next 30-60 days.

Contact your local SBA office for details.

PERSONAL PROPERTY

As you learn more about bankruptcies, estate sales, IRS, and other tax sales you will quickly notice another fantastic opportunity available to you. At these auctions you have the opportunity to acquire all sorts of personal property at rock bottom prices. For just pennies on the dollar you will be able to pick up cars, boats, bicycles, furniture, appliances, and other merchandise, including inventory from businesses that have gone belly up.

Although the main focus of this book is to show you how to pick up foreclosures and distressed real estate, you also have the potential to make lots and lots of money buying and selling personal property. What makes this so enticing is that the cost is so cheap. For example, if you buy a $1,000 computer for $30 you may turn around and resale it for $300. The buyer gets a fantastic deal and you earn ten times your investment.

This merchandise is confiscated to pay legal judgments, taxes, or debts. Some of it was confiscated by law enforcement agencies or abandoned and never claimed. Storage facilities are always selling property left in the storage units after renters stop making payments. Thousands of businesses and individuals file for bankruptcy. Their property and inventory are auctioned off to pay off debtors. There is always people and businesses that go into distress and assets must be liquidated, but in a depressed economy the numbers increase, providing investors a wealth of undervalued merchandise to choose from.

Merchandise auction ads.

The court will appoint a trustee whose job is to liquidate assets of the debtor to pay creditors. The trustee is not that concerned about getting a fair market price on the items being sold. He is primarily concerned with liquidating all the assets as quickly as possible. Because of this, you can pick up some excellent deals.

As you can imagine the type of merchandise available includes virtually anything from binoculars, luggage and tools to watches and jewelry. Merchandise is usually sold at a fraction of its value. You may buy items for ten cents on the dollar. An item that may be valued at $20 and you may pay only $2. You can turn around and resell these items at retail or wholesale and make a big profit.

Where can you sell this merchandise? Many stores would be willing to buy inexpensive inventory. The best outlet, perhaps, is a flea market. Many of the people who sell at flea markets get their merchandise this way. If you don't want to work the flea market yourself, you can resell to another merchant at wholesale and still make a killing.

People like flea markets because they feel they get merchandise at discounted prices, and usually they do. If you buy a pair of $20 sunglasses at auction for $2 and resell it for $18 at a flea market you earn $16. If you sell the sunglasses to another dealer for $10, you will still make an $8 profit. But you won't just sell a single pair of glasses, you will sell many of them. You will buy a case of 100 sunglasses at $2 each or $200 total. Resell them to a dealer at $10 each for $1,000. That would leave you with $800 profit. If you did this with several items you can see how you can make lots and lots of money. If you had the desire and time you could sell them directly to the public yourself and earn $1,600—and this is with just one item.

The type and amount of merchandise available increases every time an economic recession hits. You are about to face a golden opportunity to acquire loads of valuable property in the coming years at next to nothing. There will be so much and such a variety available to you that you will not have to worry about competition. The nice thing about reselling this type of merchandise is that at flea markets the customers hope to get products at discount prices. That's why they go there. A 10 or 20 percent discount off the retail price gives the customer a break but still leaves a healthy profit for the dealer. In slow economic times more people, conscious of keeping a tight budget, will look for good deals and head out to flea markets. So there will always be plenty of customers.

Even if you don't pursue real estate you can reap big profits from bankruptcy sales as well as the other sales described later in this chapter. If you have the time, you can make flea market selling a very profitable business for yourself.

Many people travel from city to city picking up merchandise for pennies on the dollar. Its a very simple process that anybody can do.

Many auctions are advertised in the newspaper under "Legal Notices" in the classified section. Better yet, is to get on the government agencies or auctioneer's mailing list so you're informed of each sale.

Buying and selling personal property is excellent way to earn money. If you don't have much money now, it is a good way to build up cash so you can invest it in foreclosures and distressed real estate. More information on setting up this type of business is covered in Chapter 9.

6

BUYING DISTRESSED PROPERTIES

If you're looking for a bargain on a used automobile where would you look? Happy Jacks Used Auto Sales? No, a dealer is the last place to go. The best deals are usually directly from the car's owner. A car sold by the owner may not always be a good deal however. Logically, an owner who is not in any rush to sell, can and will hold on to the car until someone comes along who will pay the asking price.

If, on the other hand, the seller is in need of quick cash and needs to sell the car as fast as possible, he will likely give it away for merely a song and dance.

Buying homes operates in the same way. If you can locate a property ready to go into foreclosure, you have a chance to buy it at a price even lower than what you could at a foreclosure auction. A home that is owned by someone who is in debt and having trouble making payments and with a very real possibly of going into foreclosure is referred to a *distressed property*. In this chapter you will learn how to buy property like this before it reaches the foreclosure sale.

A $54,000 PROFIT

By now you are aware of the great potential in buying and selling foreclosed real estate. In this chapter I'm going to show you how to make a lot more money and at a much lower financial risk to you. Buying distressed property is the cheapest and quickest way to obtain real estate. You don't need much money nor do you need to be able to qualify for a loan. Just about anyone can do and make a killing. Let me illustrate what I mean with an experience a friend of mine had.

Several years ago he decided to buy some investment property. He and a partner found a good deal on a home located just off the beach in Galveston, Texas, purchased it, and began renting it out. He had done so well with obtaining this property that he began looking for other properties. The two of them bought five more homes. After awhile, they decided to break the part-

nership and divide the homes. My friend received three and his partner received three. One of the homes that went with his partner was that first one in Galveston.

Several years passed and his former partner sold the Galveston home. The new owner eventually suffered some financial problems which lead him to pick up stakes and abandon the property.

Soon after, my friend, upon opening up his mail, found a delinquency notice on the Galveston house. As far as the mortgage company was concerned, he was still the owner of that house and still obligated to pay off the loan. This put him into a bind. Legally he was obligated to pay it off, but he had no desire to keep it and his former partner had since died. Sounds like a dime novel, doesn't it? But it's true.

While trying to decide what he was going to do, the mortgage company sent him notice that they were going to accelerate his loan, thus making the entire loan amount due. The balance left on the loan was $16,000. An appraisal on the home gave it a value of almost $70,000. All he had to do in order to keep this $70,000 home was to pay off the $16,000. He recognized it as an ideal investment, but he didn't have $16,000 in cash and really wasn't in the position to borrow it at the time. He did not want to keep the property and as far as he was concerned, he would have let the mortgage company keep it, but in so doing his credit record could be damaged, something he didn't want.

Knowing that this would be a good investment for someone wanting to buy a home, he mentioned his situation to people he thought might be interested in such an investment. He told these people that if they went to the mortgage company, they could pay the $16,000 balance on the note and in effect take over the lien. He would then sign over a deed to the property with the stipulation that he be relieved from making any further payment on the note.

One of his friends took him up on the deal, phoned the mortgage company, and explained that he wanted to purchase the note on this particular piece of property. The clerk whom he was talking to, in typical fashion answered, "Oh, we don't do that," and thus ended the conversation and the transaction.

Later, an elderly lady phoned my friend and asked him if he was indeed trying to sell this property and could she get it for only $16,000. She had the cash and wanted to purchase a new home if it was still available. "Yes it was," he replied and gave her all the particulars. He told her "Don't phone the mortgage company because the clerks who answer the phone don't know how to handle the situation." He told her instead to write out a check for $16,000 and send a letter with it asking to take possession of the note.

That's what she did, and a few days later she received the note signed over to her in the mail. My friend then signed a deed of ownership to her. If she had turned around and sold the property for its appraised value, she would have realized a $54,000 profit.

CASHING IN ON DISTRESSED REAL ESTATE

The story above illustrates an exceptionally good deal, but this type of thing goes on all the time. Let me give you a fictionalized but more typical example.

Mr. and Mrs. Haveahouse were facing some financial difficulties that made their mortgage payments an extreme burden. Mr. Haveahouse had kept current on his payments but was seriously considering walking away from the home. The thought of destroying his credit was the only thing that kept him from doing it.

One day he noticed a sign posted on a fence which read, "I Buy Homes-Call 713-IBUY."

"Maybe I could sell it," he thought. "That would be better then dumping the house in the lender's lap."

He called the number to see what type of deal he could get. The potential buyer, Mr. Will R. Dealer, came over to look at the house.

"I'll give you $500 to assume your loan and take over payments, if you deed the property to me," he said.

Mr. Haveahouse thought about that for a moment. "I was considering leaving the home to the lender for nothing, but this person will give me $500 cash and save my credit . . . I'll do it."

Will Dealer hands him a quitclaim deed* which the Haveahouses sign, conveying their ownership of the property to him. Relieved that their credit

---

*A quitclaim deed is a simple document that transfers any or all ownership of the property from the homeowner to a second party. It contains no warranties or covenants but is just a simple transfer of ownership. It should be witnessed and notarized but does not have to be, nor does it require a lawyer. Quitclaim deeds can be purchased from most office supply stores. The critical phrase in this document is the statement that the seller "does hereby quitclaim" or something to that effect. The term quitclaim means to renounce all ownership, rights or interest in the property. See the sample quitclaim deed on page 69.

will be protected and happy to get even $500 out of the deal, the Haveahouses pack up and leave. Mr. Dealer now has two options he can rent the house out at a price sufficient to cover the mortgage payment plus a little more, or he can turn around and resell it. If he rents it he will receive a monthly pay check for as long as the home is rented. The property also appreciates in value. If he turns around and resells it immediately he can cash in the equity of the home, which may amount to $10,000, $20,000, or more.

His only outlay was the initial $500 and any back payments the Haveahouse's didn't may have missed paying. It's all perfectly legal and done every day by hundreds of people. The beauty of it all is that you can do it too. It takes no great deal of real estate or legal knowledge. All you need is a warranty or quitclaim deed ready to be signed.

If you want to really get some good deals in real estate, this is absolutely the best way to go. You don't even have to go through the hassle of getting a loan and don't even have to be able to qualify for one. If your credit is bad or income too low to qualify for a mortgage on the size of property you would like, you can side step getting a loan by using this method. It is even possible to have the seller sign the property over to you without you making a cash payment. That's right, no payment whatsoever.

Why would somebody sell a home under these conditions? The promise to take over the mortgage payments, save his credit, and relieve him of the mental anguish of foreclosure may be enough, but money is a factor too. Selling a home costs money. The listing fee alone with the real estate broker may be as much as $1,500. His commission will run five or six thousand dollars. If you have a prepayment penalty written in on your mortgage that's another five or six thousand dollars that will go to the lender. Some of the closing costs may also be required by the seller. Selling a moderately priced home may cost $10,000 or more!

If the homeowner is pressed for money, he's not going to have this much lying around. Of course, most of these fees can be taken out of the selling price of the property, but if the owner doesn't have over $10,000 or $15,000 in equity, he'll have to dig some money out of his pocket just to sell and get rid of the house. Besides, there is no guarantee that the home would even sell. If it sells for less or not at all, the homeowner stands to lose. Just getting rid of the property without suffering more loss than is necessary makes these deals good for both buyer and seller

If you desire, you could purchase the home in the traditional manner by bringing in a lender to finance it for you. The only drawback to this is that both of you will be paying these extra fees which the lender will charge. If the loan can be assumed, most of these expenses will be eliminated.

Government insured loans are fully assumable and being such, do not require exorbitant closing costs to transfer title, nor do they contain prepayment penalties. Conventional loans, on the other hand, almost always contain

QUITCLAIM DEED

THE STATE OF Texas

KNOW ALL MEN BY THESE PRESENTS:

COUNTY OF Harris

That Fred and Martha Homer

of the County of Harris ,State of Texas , for and

in consideration of the sum of Five hundred and no/100 DOLLARS in hand

paid by the grantee herein named, the receipt of which is hereby acknowledged, have QUITCLAIMED,

and by these presents do QUITCLAIM unto John Smith

of the County of Harris ,State of Texas ,all of their right,

title and interest in and to the following described real property situated in Harris County,

Texas , to-wit: Lot one, Block one, Sunny Acres Subdivision.

TO HAVE AND TO HOLD all of our right, title and interest in and to the above described property

and premises unto the said grantees, their heirs and assigns forever, so that neither we nor

our heirs, legal representatives or assigns shall have, claim or demand any right or title to the

aforesaid property, premises or appurtenances or any part thereof.

EXECUTED this 15th day of June , A.D. 2000

_____   _____

THE STATE OF TEXAS, COUNTY OF HARRIS

Before me, the undersigned authority, on this day personally appeared Fred Homer and Martha Homer

known to me to be the persons whose name(s) are subscribed to the foregoing instrument, and

acknowledged to me that they executed the same for the purposes and consideration therein expressed.

Given under my hand and seal of office on this the 15th day of June , A.D. 2000

_____
Notary Public

Sample quitclaim deed.

a due-on-sale clause, which requires the seller to pay off the total amount of the loan when it is sold or refinanced. In this way, the lenders can charge for full closing costs, prepayment penalties, and possibly increase the interest rate. To avoid the hassles lenders cause, you can legally keep them out of the process until the transfer has already taken place.

ASSUMABLE AND NONASSUMABLE MORTGAGES

In an ordinary real estate transaction the seller is given a certain amount of money for his property. With this money, the old mortgage is paid in full and becomes void. The buyer pays for the purchase of the property with a new loan and becomes responsible for a new mortgage. This process involves numerous fees and closing costs that can amount to three to six percent of the loan amount equaling several thousand dollars. Banks make a rich profit off these fees and so insist on them whenever possible.

There is no law that requires the lenders involvement in buying or selling real estate. Years ago all home mortgages were assumable, that is, if a some-one bought a home he also assumed responsibility of paying off the original mortgage on the home. All FHA and VA insured loans are still fully assumable. But lenders have added due-on-sale clauses to most conventional home loans which states that whenever the property changes hands the loan becomes due and must be paid in full. This way the lender can charge an array of closing fees and jack up the interest rate.

By finding property with assumable mortgages you can side step the lender and deal only with the homeowner. A real estate broker is also unnecessary, saving the seller an additional 6 percent of the total sales price that would go as the broker's commission.

Normally, the lender would want to know when any type of transaction like this occurs so he can muscle in on the act. The original mortgage may have a prepayment penalty attached to it, requiring the former owner to pay a few thousand dollars if the loan is paid off early. Or perhaps it is a conventional loan which may not be assumable.

If the property you have purchased was insured by the FHA or VA, then the loan is fully assumable. For minimum expense you can take over payments and have the note and obligation to pay put your name. The lender can't do anything about it.

If the home has a conventional mortgage however, you may need to do some negotiating. The mortgagee may or may not let you assume the loan and may want you to pay all the ordinary closing costs. Tell him "Look, either let me take over the payments as they are or foreclose. I've got nothing to lose, and the former owner has already moved out."

Remember, he will likely lose money if he tries to foreclose, but you stand to lose only what you paid the original owner, which may have been nothing. It's not likely he will let you assume the loan, but he will be interested in giving you a new loan on the property. Although certainly not as desirable as assuming the original mortgage, it may not be such a bad deal if you work it right. Your first goal is to eliminate as many of the closing costs as possible.

When discussing this with the mortgagee, do not become threatening or overbearing, act as business-like and professional as possible. He will be inclined to work out something with you if you are friendly and courteous. If you can't get the lender to give you a new note without paying some closing costs, try to make them as minimal as possible. You should discuss this with the lender and work out the details *before* you actually pay the owner and sign the deed. If the lender is uncooperative, you may want to pass on this one and look elsewhere. Never sign a deed, especially if it is nonassumable, without first talking with the lender. If he is going to be uncooperative, you don't want to deal with him.

If the loan isn't assumable you can still negotiate a favorable loan and acquire the property even if you do have to pay closing costs. When you work up a new loan you are in a very strong bargaining position. The lender doesn't want a foreclosure on his hands and will do almost anything to prevent that. You can make changes to the new loan to get more favorable terms like eliminating a due-on-sale clause, lowering the interest rate, structuring a graduated payment mortgage or balloon mortgage, or some other type of loan. It is amazing what you can get if you negotiate. You can even get all the equity out of the home immediately when the loan is set up. In this chapter our focus is on buying property directly from the homeowner and thus side stepping the lender's involvement. Working with lenders and negotiating home mortgages is covered in Chapter 7.

HOW TO FIND DISTRESSED PROPERTY

Using Your Eyes and Ears

People in financial distress don't intentionally announce the fact that they are having difficulties or that their home may soon go into foreclosure. So where do you find such people? You have to look for them. There are several ways to about finding them.

The simplest method of locating these properties is to keep your eyes on the lookout wherever you go. As you drive around town look for abandoned homes. They are easy to spot because they are usually unkempt, with abundant weeds and uncut grass, empty garages etc. Look in the windows and see if furnishings are missing.

If the owners have moved out, how do you contact them? There are several ways you can track them down. When most people move they remain in the same city or a nearby community. So, you will be able to contact them and work out a deal. But how do you find out where they went? Talk to the neighbors and see if they know the owner's new address or phone number. Explain that you are interested in buying the property. If they have any information they will likely give it to you. If you can't find the new address or phone number from the neighbors, at least get the owner's name. If you can't get that, look on their mail box. Names are often put on the mail box. Sometimes the postal carrier will stick a card in the box with the resident's last name. You may even find an old letter still sitting there with the information.

If you can get a phone number from the neighbors, great. If not, call directory assistance. If they have moved somewhere locally they most likely have a phone. Give them a call.

If you can't get hold of the owners by phone then you can try writing a letter to them. If you can get a current address that is best, but if you can't, send the letter to the old address. If they are having their mail forwarded, it will get to them. Tell them you are interested in buying the property, give your name, address, and phone number. If they didn't leave a forwarding address, the letter will be returned to you. To get quicker results you can go directly to the Post Office. For a nominal fee the Post Office will look up the new address for you, if the owners submitted a change of address form.

A home doesn't have to be abandoned for the owner to be in financial distress or threatened with foreclosure. A home that is still being lived in, but is unkempt is a sign that the owner is having financial difficulty. Once the owner stops making payments and is aware that he might lose the home he also loses interest in keeping the property up. Certainly not all unkempt homes are headed for foreclosure, often rental properties not well kept. If the homeowners are still there, you can talk to them in person. Knock on the door and ask the owner if he or she has any interest in selling the home.

If no one is home, you will want to find out the owner's name and possibly phone number. If there is no name on the mailbox or outside of the house, as before, you might try asking the neighbors. If you still can't get a name, write down the address. Go to your library and find a directory called *Hines Criss Cross Directory*. The librarian will help you locate it. This directory lists names, addresses and telephone numbers of all the homes and businesses in a particular area. If you have the address, you can look it up in the directory and it will give you the name and phone number of the owner. If you library doesn't have this book or if you would like to have access to your own copy you can get one through the publisher at Hines Criss Cross Directory, 8050 Freedom Ave. N.W., North Canton, OH 44720. Phone 216-494-9111.

Many homeowners desperate to save their credit rating and salvage some or any of their equity attempt to sell their property before it is foreclosed on.

These people will have a sign up in their yard which says, "For Sale by Owner." Avoid signs put up by Century 21 or other real estate agencies. Generally, owners sell their own property to save on the expense of using agents. Many times they are low on cash and can't really afford such an expense. The listing fee alone may be $1,500. Of course, not all homes advertised as for sale by owner will be distressed property. The large majority will not. But you can talk to the owner and see what the situation is.

Elements of psychology come into play when a homeowner attempts to sell his own home as is evidenced in the size of the for sale sign he sticks in his front yard. A big sign means the owner is fed up with something; he's selling due to emotional reasons more then anything else. He may give you a good deal, or he may just want the opportunity to sound off while refusing any reasonable offer.

A small sign means the owner is in some financial difficulty and needs to sell the home quickly. He is somewhat self-conscience about this fact so the sign he uses is small, hoping that the neighbors may not notice so easily. This type of person can give you the bargain you've been looking for. Judging the owner by the size of the for sale sign is, of course, a generality, but none the less has some element of truth.

Talk to friends, neighbors, relatives, and business associates. What do you talk about? Real estate. Also ask if they know of anyone who is getting a divorce and if they want to sell their house. Some of the best deals will come simply by word of mouth.

If you hand out your business card and let everyone you meet know you invest in foreclosed and distressed property and can help people avoid foreclosure, people will call you. You may give your card to car dealer, who may have a brother-in-law who is having financial troubles, he will pass your name to him. So, even if the person you give your card to doesn't seem like a likely candidate for you, he may know someone who is.

As you get more involved in this business and begin talking to others, you will invariably hear about homes that are being foreclosed on or in trouble. Follow up on these leads.

Real Estate Professionals

Often, when people realize they may lose their home they try to do the most logical thing they can think of and that is to sell the property. They contact a Realtor and see if there is any way they can sell it. Time is running out on them and they are desperate. Some agents will try to help, but most realize that their chances are not good. Often, the owner won't be able to pay the listing fee.

The owner will want to sell at a price that will cover the Realtor's commission and recoup as much equity as possible. But to sell quickly the house must be discounted and discounted enough to make it enticing to buyers even after the buyer pays off back payments. The property must still have enough equity to pay for the Realtor's commission. Distressed property, however, is not attractive to most home buyers because if notice has been placed at the county courthouse it will show up in records as legal action taking place, and most buyers don't want to get involved. Few people know how to handle property facing foreclosure so most people will distance themselves. Because of the above conditions most Realtors won't be able to do much to help troubled homeowners.

You can call real estate agents and ask if you know of any property in this situation. They may lead you to people they could not help. If you can develop a good relationship with some Realtors they can provide you with tips they receive in their normal process of business. You might even consider offering a referral fee to motivate them to give you these tips. This fee may be based on every referral or just on those that you are able to buy. You might offer a small fee for every lead and a larger fee if you are able to make a deal with the homeowner. You can work out anything that is satisfactory between you.

You might consider doing something similar with attorneys. They are contacted by homeowners seeking assistance in saving their home. These leads can be passed to you. One of the best ways for a homeowner to avoid going through a foreclosure is to sell the property. A lawyer who has a resource, an investor who is willing to consider this option, can provide a valuable service to such people. He doesn't have to refer you to his client necessarily, but he can pass on information to you. He can also keep you aware of any restrictions or liens on the property or the existing loan.

Foreclosure Reports

When property goes into foreclosure lenders must file them at the courthouse. These courthouse records are open to the public so you can go look them up. Ask the clerks and they will show you what to do. You will be shown books with lists of names and addresses of those whose loans are in default and foreclosure pending. Since the foreclosure process usually takes four to six months, if you get the names early enough you have plenty of time to approach the homeowner, evaluate the property, and make an offer.

An easier way to get a list of pending foreclosures is to subscribe to a foreclosure report. Subscription information is often posted on the bulletin board at the county courthouse. The clerks that work with these records may also know if any such publication is available in your area.

Foreclosure reports or newsletters are complied by someone who does just exactly what I explained to you. He goes in on a regular basis and records all new foreclosure listings and complies them in a little report. This report may be printed every week or every month depending on the number of foreclosures in your area. A subscription will cost you some money, but it will save you a lot of time. The only drawback to the report is that if you wait for the report to find properties, then other investors who also subscribe to the publication will learn about them at the same time you do. You may have some competition. This hasn't been too much of a problem in the past because not too many people do this and there are often lots of properties available. Cost ranges from about $50 to $300 a year for subscription.

Another source is your local legal newspaper. This paper lists all legal actions occurring in your area. It may list pending foreclosures and foreclosure auctions.

The legal newspaper will also provide you with many leads to people who are undergoing financial crises. Most will not be in foreclosure yet, but may soon be or at least be considering it.

Look up any court judgments against people who will owe a lot of money. Better yet, you will find a list of those filing for divorce. This could be a rich resource for you. Divorces cause a lot of financial upheavals and homes are often quickly sold in the process. The listing usually includes the name and address of both parties. Write them a letter and tell them you buy real estate, "I am sorry your life is being disrupted by divorce. At this time you may be looking to sell your home. I am a real estate investor and would like to discuss the possibility of buying your property." Keep it short and to the point, one or two paragraphs is enough. Not everyone you send it to will respond, but some will. Buy this time they are talking to their friends saying, "If I could just get rid of this house, I'd be out of here."

Divorce is an ugly situation. Most people tend to refrain from talking about it to those who are involved because they don't want to appear like they're prying in someone else's private affairs. So how do you approach the situation? Keep in mind that divorces are not secret, they are public knowledge just as bankruptcies or name changes are and as such are published in legal or local newspapers. You have a right to this information so don't think that you're prying into people's lives. When you approach the couple do it in a business-like manner.

Your Approach

When you approach someone and discuss a sensitive subject, how do you do it without the fear of offending them or appearing to be nosy? The first thing to keep in mind is that you're not interested in their personal problems. You are there to offer a business deal, so act professional and business-like, just like a life insurance or any other respectable salesman would. But unlike a salesman, your not selling anything, you're trying to buy something. I would much rather talk to someone who is trying to buy something from me than one who is trying to sell me something.

A simple telephone call is the cheapest and most time efficient method of contacting the owner. Introduce yourself, giving your name and the business or company you represent. Simply state that your company is looking for property in the neighborhood. Would he be interested in selling his home. If not, ask if he knows of anyone else who wants to sell their property.

Keep in mind, that the owner may or may not be in financial trouble. Your letter may read something like the following:

Dear Mr. and Mrs. Homeowner:

My name is Frank Snorkel I represent Blue Sky Real Estate Investments. We have been purchasing properties in your area for several years. As real estate professionals, we are able to quickly analyze your property and make a qualified purchase offer to you within a matter of days. We are able to pay all cash or to assume existing financing.

If you would have an interest in exploring the possibilities of selling your property, I would be very interested in setting up a time to come meet with you.

I look forward to hearing from you soon.

Sincerely,

Frank Snorkel

If the homeowner has already moved out of the home or you know the homeowner is in default (from courthouse records) and is about to lose his home you may want to be more direct.

Dear Mr. and Mrs. Homeowner:

Are financial problems troubling you? Do you need quick cash to pay off bills and protect your property from foreclosure? If so, we have a solution that may be of help to you.

My name is Frank Snorkel. I represent Blue Sky Real Estate Investments. Our business is buying and selling investment properties.

As a real estate investment company we keep track of all legal proceedings occurring in the county. Your property was recently listed as being in foreclosure. This is a serious situation because if steps aren't taken soon, you risk losing your home and destroying your credit record. We can help you out.

If your property meets our criteria, we may be able to buy it from you for cash, and pay off all overdue payments, interest, and legal fees on your property. You will be able stop the foreclosure process, protect your credit rating, and walk away with cash in hand.

I must emphasize that time is limited. The longer you delay doing something, the more it will cost in late fees and penalties to prevent the foreclosure and the less money you may possibly get for your property. If you wait too long, it will be beyond our power to prevent foreclosure. So, I encourage you to act now by giving me a call at 555-3543. We can find a solution for you.

Sincerely,

Frank Snorkel

Getting Them to Come to You

The best way to find distressed property is to get the homeowners come to you. One way to do this is to put up signs which read: "I Buy Homes", "Will Buy Your Home Today", " I Buy Homes, Fast and Fair", "Cash For Your Property", "Save Your Home From Foreclosure", "Cash For Your Equity", "I Buy Real Estate", or something similar. Include your phone number and let people contact you. Put notices up at launderette bulletin boards, supermarkets, fences, and anywhere you can. Financially troubled homeowners, desperate for help, will find you. Some foreclosure investors claim they get most of their business this way.

You might also try placing ads in the newspaper. Have the ad placed under "Real Estate Wanted" section. Here are a few examples of what you can say.

"Avoid foreclosure—save good credit! Will assume your payments. Quick action."

"I buy houses, any area, any condition."

"Are you trying to sell your assumable home and don't want any equity? I guarantee I can sell your home regardless of payments or interest in 20 days or less or I will personally buy it!"

You may try looking in the classified ads for people trying to sell their own property. Look for ads which say "For Sale By Owner" or "Must Sacrifice." Be careful though, some clever real estate agents place these "Must sell" ads to attract prospects.

BUYING PROPERTY BEFORE THE FORECLOSURE SALE

The Homeowner's Dilemma

By buying property that is on the verge of going into foreclosure you can make a lot of money. The down side of this business is that you must deal with people who are struggling financially. It's because of their problems that this opportunity even exists.

Sometimes people may question the ethics of buying homes for a few hundred or few thousand dollars, especially when they are financially in trouble and on the verge of losing their home. In reality, what you are doing is answering their prayers. You are actually helping them out. You are not taking an unfair advantage of someone in a bad situation, you are providing a way for them to escape many of the horrible consequences of going through a foreclosure.

When you purchase properties from people who have no way to paying their debts, you are giving them a way out before things get even worse. By purchasing the property before it goes into foreclosure, you pay off the back payments and fees, releasing them of a heavy financial obligation they can't afford. They are able to honorably and legally sell the property to you and acquire much needed cash. If the property went into foreclosure the former owner would not only lose the home, but would get no money at all. In fact, he may very well face a deficiency judgment and owe money. By selling to you the homeowner avoids paying a Realtor. He also protects his credit. These are very import considerations for the homeowner to make.

At this point, the homeowner has no other recourse. He may have tried to refinance or get a second mortgage but could not quality for the loan. He may not have been able to list the home for sale with a Realtor because the Realtor's listing fee and commission would be far more than he could afford. And once the home has defaulted, it is recorded and any prospective buyer will find out that the home is under legal action and this is enough to scare most potential buyers away. They don't want to be involved in any legal entanglements. In order to buy the home they will be expected to pay all fees accumulated. Most people just don't want to get involved. When you buy these homes you help the homeowner, the lender, and yourself. It's a win-win-win situation.

Determining Value

It's important that when you find a distressed property to complete your evaluation and do all you need to as quickly as possible. Once the foreclosure clock is ticking the property can go into foreclosure before you or the homeowner realize it. Then it's too late. The only way for you to purchase the property is at the foreclosure auction. Also, every month the homeowner withholds payment, late fees and penalties mount up, which you will be required to pay off if you buy the home. So the longer you wait the more it will cost you.

Once you've made the initial contact with the homeowners, set up an appointment with them to discuss the possibility of buying their home. If the property is jointly owned it is best to talk to both.

In this meeting find out how much they owe in back payments, the loan amount, lender's name, etc. Find out if they have a second or third mortgage and how much is owed and if they've missed payments to them as well. You say to them, "Tell me all the loans you have on the property. I'm going to buy it on condition that what you tell me is true." Owners desperate to find a buyer may not tell you everything to avoid scaring you away. Regardless of what they tell you, before signing the contract and finalizing the purchase, have a title company run a title report, this will reveal all liens against the property. It will cost you a couple of hundred dollars but may save your neck. You will need to factor this and other expenses into your calculations when determining if the property will bring you enough profit to make it worth your time.

You won't make an offer at this first meeting with the owners. Your initial visit is to see how open they are to selling the home and to gather information and examine the property. When you inspect the house do it very carefully and point out everything you see wrong with the property. Every house has things wrong with it. This will help them know the house isn't worth full market value as it is, and that repairs will cost them too much. After examining the property and getting all the information you need, if the house looks promising, tell the owners that you will check on the information they gave you and get back in touch with them in a couple of days. Then leave. Don't discuss price and don't ask them how much they want for the house. They will always quote you a figure comparable to the current market value. But you don't pay market value for property. You will come back to them with an offer if the property has enough equity to make it worth your time.

Now is the time to do your homework. Call the trustee and find out what you need to do to cure the loan and stop the foreclosure process. You need to find out the exact amount that it will take to cure it. Keep in mind this figure may increase by the time you have made a deal with the owner and are ready to take action.

Go to the bank or call and find out the exact loan balance, the monthly payments, and if there will be any changes made to the loan if you take it over. Talk to loan officer and tell him what you are doing. Work out an arrangement that allows you to bring current all the late payments and penalties as well as paying off any other liens on the property. He will be willing to help you because you represent a possible solution to his problem.

At this point, if everything looks good you need to go to a title company or to the courthouse and look at the title status of the property. Check the homeowner's name to see if there are any liens against him that might cause a problem.

Once you've gathered the above information, you must calculate everything owed on the home and subtract it from the current market value to establish the equity in the home. I recommend that the property have at least $15,000 minimum for you to even consider it.

Let's go through an example. Say you estimate the market value for a particular home at $100,000. The amount owed the lender is $75,000. The equity in the home is $25,000.

You have $25,000 to work with to determine if this property will be worth your time and expense.

You must factor in all your expenses in obtaining and reselling the property. In order to prevent the foreclosure you will need to pay all back payments, late fees, penalties, and legal expenses. If you buy the home early in the foreclosure process you may end up paying only a couple thousand dollars for this. But if the foreclosure has been pending for several months it may cost you $4,000 or $5,000 or more. You need to call the lender and find out exactly how much you will need to pay them to cure the loan. Tell them what you're doing and they will be happy to work with you. They don't want the property back and will be glad to have you take over the loan. For our example, let's say the home is in the final stages of a pending foreclosure and several months of past due payments and penalties have accumulated so that you need $5,000 to cure the loan.

Add another $600 for title search, recording, and legal fees.

Now let's consider expenses to sell the property. You will need to clean the property and fix it up to resell. This will include yard work and some repairs that may cost you $1,000. Add on to that another $400 for marketing and advertising.

Your total expenses come to $7,000. Keep in mind that I am purposely calculating expense on the *high* side so you will know how much it can cost. But your expenses can be much less, perhaps only $1,000-$2,000 total.

Subtract $7,000 from the equity in the home and you're left with $18,000. This is the maximum amount of profit you can expect if you sell the home at market value and if you didn't pay anything to the owner for the property.

The question you need to ask yourself now is how much profit do you want to make? I would shoot for a minimum of $15,000. I like to have this much because it makes the whole process worthwhile. Also, you may want to sell the home at a discount in order to get a quick sale. The discount may be $5,000 to $8,000 so that would leave you with only a few thousand dollars in profit.

If you set you minimum profit margin at $15,000 that leaves you with $3,000 out of the $18,000 to work with the owner. You can offer the owner the full $3,000 or a lessor amount. You don't even need to offer any money. Just taking over the loan and relieving him the financial obligation may be enough. In most cases, you would offer at least $500 or $2,000. This is enough money for them to move out and set up somewhere else.

Second Mortgages and Other Liens

One of the things you must be aware of when purchasing distressed property is the presence of a second mortgage or other liens. When you assume ownership you also assume responsibility of the mortgage and any other liens on the property. A second mortgage may easily wipe out any equity in the property. You could possibly own more than what the property is worth. It may have been one of the reasons why the former owners wanted to unload the property.

If you buy property at a foreclosure auction, there is little to worry about. Once the property has completed the foreclosure process and is actually sold at auction, all the liens will be abolished. You would get a deed to the property free and clear and not one other lien holder would have recourse against you.

The only exception is if there are government liens such as for property taxes or income tax. These liens stay with the property.

If you, as an investor, purchase a home at anytime before it goes to the foreclosure sale, you will be getting it for just the back payments and whatever you pay the former owner, but you will also be assuming any other current liabilities.

You need to find if there are any liens against the property. There are numerous ways that a property could have liens put against it. In some cases the owner might not even know about a lien against him or the property.

There are five types of liens. When a property is subject to more than one lien, priority is established by the type of lien and by the date of its recording. The priority from top to bottom is as follows:

(1) Tax liens. This includes real estate tax, federal estate, state inheritance and federal income tax, and state intangible tax liens.

(2) Mortgage liens. Used as security on home loans.

(3) Vendor liens. A vender may subject the property as security for any unpaid principal balance of debt.

(4) Mechanics' liens. Is a lien for labor, materials, supplies, or repairs to construct or improve the property.

(5) Judgment liens. Is awarded against a defendant as a result of a lawsuit.

If you try to buy the property before the foreclosure sale, or rather the cure date which may be some days before the sale, you will inherit any liens or judgments on the property as well. A proper title search will uncover all of these. Any title company can do this for you. Although a home may have other liens besides the first mortgage, that doesn't mean it may not be a good deal. You need to consider the total amount and take that into account when figuring the profit potential for the property. Small liens can be added in to your expenses and still leave enough for you to enjoy a sizable profit.

Let's look a situation where the owner has more than one loan. Assume the home has a fair market value of $100,000. The balance on the first mortgage is $65,000 and the balance on the second mortgage is $10,000. For simplicity let's assume the same expense described in the previous example so we must add an additional $7,000. In this example, you must add the second mortgage amount to the expenses. So total expense amounts to $17,000. Since the home has $35,000 in equity that leaves you with $18,000, the same amount as in the first example. So, even though a home may have a second or even a third mortgage it may still be a good investment. You can't judge until you've gone though the calculations.

Often homes that go into foreclosure have liens of some sort. Homeowners struggling with financial problems frequently take out second or third mortgages to pay off debts and find themselves deeper in trouble than they were before. If they have been strapped for money they may not have paid debts which then end up as liens on their home. When figuring the amount you are willing to invest, you must also figure in any liens that will need to be paid.

If a first mortgage is not being paid, it's a good guess that the second isn't either. Go to the second lien holder and explain that the owner is having financial difficulty. He, of course, will already be aware of this fact because he hasn't been getting paid. Tell him you are willing to pay cash for the note if he will sell it to you at a discount. You might be able to buy if for half its face value. If there is $10,000 owed you might get it for $5,000. This will reduce the amount you will have to pay by $5,000. You just earned $5,000! This is relatively easy when the second mortgage is owned by a business or individual as opposed to a bank.

Often, the second mortgage is owned by an individual. This is much more common nowadays than it was in the past. Banks are less willing to negotiate, but it doesn't hurt to try. It may be well worth your time. The bank many sell you the note at only a $1,000 or $2,000 discount. Even at this you earn $1,000 or $2,000 more than you would otherwise.

Once the quitclaim deed is signed, is there any turning back? After the signing of the deed you discover something to your disliking, if you have not yet paid the lender and had it recorded, you can cancel the agreement by tearing up the deed. Since you have not been recorded as the owner, the property reverts back to the original owner. Make sure you tell the owner what has happened and cancel it or tear it up in his presence. This isn't a vengeful thing, just a matter of business to let them know he is still responsible for the mortgage. This kind of situation might occur if there is some type of provision in the original mortgage that would prevent you from acquiring the land as you expected or make it undesirable to do so. For this reason, it is advisable to talk to the lender as soon after the deed is signed as possible. If you've given the former owner a check in payment and he will not or can not refund the money, go to your bank immediately and have them cancel payment on the check. It may cost you $20 or so, but may save you much more.

Negotiating with the Owners

Long before the foreclosure clock starts ticking and before a legal announcement is placed in the newspaper, the homeowner knows he is in danger of losing his property. He may have been struggling for some time. He may have kept up payments but be hanging on by his fingertips, or he may only be one or two months behind. The possibility of losing his home is in his mind. At this point, many homeowners will listen to you and consider your offer, especially in the light that it may save their credit rating and avoid deficiency judgment and embarrassment. The owner is facing a very realistic possibly of losing his home, ruining his credit without receiving any compensation what so ever, and may still be required to fork up some cash in the process. Its an ugly situation. You can help him escape from his turmoil and perhaps give him enough money to get him established elsewhere.

After working out your profit margin you know exactly how much leeway you have in deciding on an offer. As mentioned above, in most cases you will offer somewhere between $500 and $2,000. The more equity they have the more you can offer.

At first, this amount doesn't seem like much to give for a home, and the owners may be surprised at such a low offer. But keep in mind, that you are offering much, much more than just some quick cash. You are offering to take over the responsibility of paying back their loan, wipe out their delinquent payments and late fees, protect their credit, prevent a possible deficiency judgment, and avoid the humiliation and embarrassment of going through a foreclosure. You've done a lot of work to make this offer available to them, it should be worth something to you and to them. This is an entirely fair offer on your part. If you didn't make any money from it, you couldn't even make such an offer and they would have little hope in escaping from their financial dilemma. You've offered them some hope.

You've provided the owner the only sensible option to chose from. The owner at this point should be desperate to sell, because that will be the only thing that will get him out the situation he is in, unless somebody gives him a huge chunk of money all of the sudden. The chances of that are next to zero. Most homeowners will try to hang on to their property if they can. They may try to get a home equity loan so they can keep making mortgage payments until their financial situation turns around.

The problem with getting a loan is that loans have to be paid back. If the homeowner got a loan he would incur more monthly debt and if his income didn't increase soon, he would be right back where he started. If he has defaulted on his mortgage it would be almost impossible to get another loan. No one would want to risk giving him a loan to pay off another loan.

The only option he has is to sell his property regardless of the loss he must take. If the home goes into foreclosure, no matter how much equity he has, it will most assuredly be lost and he won't see a penny of it. If he sells to you for $1,000 he would get $1,000 more than he would otherwise.

The homeowner has little negotiating power. He must sell or risk losing his house, all his equity, and ruin his credit.

You may encounter homeowners who will want to hold out, thinking they deserve full market value for the home. You cannot do this and justify your time and expense. They must bargain with you. Keep in mind, that you don't have to buy their house, but they desperately need to get out from under debt, and selling the house is the only way they can do it, even if they don't get any money from it. The longer they stay in the house the more mortgage payments they miss and the more in debt they become. The longer they delay in making a deal with you, the more it will cost you to take over the loan and the less you can offer them. They need to make a decision quickly. The time factor is very important. They don't have the time to put the house on the market and wait for someone to come along and buy it. Most prospective buyers won't want to get involved in buying a home threatened with foreclosure, so the chances that they would sell it through normal channels is nil. You are their only hope of getting out of a very nasty situation.

If you contact the homeowner before he has missed any payments he will be more difficult to work with. He may not be satisfied with getting a few hundred dollars and letting you take over the property by assuming the loan and the responsibility of paying for it. He will want more for the property. The further he heads toward foreclosure the less demanding he will be. In the early stages, you may consider offering more than you would at later stages. If you waited a few months when the homeowner is more desperate to sell, the cost to rescue the home from going through foreclosure will be greater. If it will cost $3,000 to pay off back debts owed by the homeowner in a couple of months, you might consider offering that amount to him. The cost to you will be the same either way, but the homeowner gets the cash rather than the lender. Let him know your offer is good only if he accepts it within a specified time, such as one or two weeks. Let him know that the longer he takes to decide, the more costly it will be for you to pay off his debt and take over the loan and you will decrease your offer.

To help motivate the owners to sell, you might also offer an option for them to buy the property back from you within a certain period of time. If you plan on renting the property this may be a good strategy to consider. You may even let them rent the property from you, but they must pay a rent equal or greater than the mortgage payment. This is something they may be able to do because they don't have to worry about making up back payments and penalties. Usually, when a loan goes into default the lender demands full payment of all missed payments stipulating that no partial payments would be accepted. When someone is having trouble making monthly payments they aren't likely going to have several month's worth of cash readily available. They are nearly helpless at this point. Your offer gives them time to get back on their feet.

The time period for them to redeem the property may be six months to a year or more. If they want to redeem the property they would pay you $10,000 or whatever you agree on. That may sound like an awful lot for someone who has been struggling financially, so you might want to make a slightly different offer where they can pay you a down payment and you will finance the loan. They would pay you say $3,000 down and finance the rest with you. They could either finance the remaining $7,000 ($10,000 - $3,000 = $7,000) after which you will let them assume the loan or you would resell the home to them at market value and finance the entire amount. So if the home is valued at $90,000 this is the amount they finance from you. This is a good option to consider because it can earn you both principal and interest for the life of the loan, which may be as long as 30 years. This is called a wraparound mortgage and is explained in more detail in the next chapter.

The possibility of being able to reclaim their home is a good motivator for owners who are stubborn. They likely have a lot of sentimental value in the home and this type of arrangement makes it easier for them to accept a difficult decision.

At times, you will meet homeowners who just don't realize the seriousness of the situation they are in. They feel there will be some way they will get out of the foreclosure before it happens or be able to reclaim the property quickly afterwards. These type of people will stay in their homes to the end. A bad mistake, because not only will they not sell it to you, but they may be evicted immediately after the foreclosure sale and lose all assets remaining on the property at the time of eviction. These type of people are headed for serious trouble.

You need to explain to them the seriousness of their problem and the consequences they face with eviction and confiscation of property, deficiency judgments, and such. You can help them avoid all that mess. If that doesn't motivate them to think seriously about leaving, you're wasting your time with them. Move on to other properties.

Many real estate investors will not even bother approaching a homeowner if they are still occupying the home. They will only pursue those who have already moved out. Yet, you can find many people still in their homes who will work with you, especially if and when they discover the grave consequences of staying and realize you offer them a comparatively painless way out.

If, after you discuss all the consequences and options with them and they still won't sell at your price, let it go. Leave them your business card and tell them to call you if they change their minds. Forewarn them that if they wait too long, you will need to revise your offer to account for increased expenses. Then leave.

Don't be too disappointed if you don't get the property. It's a waste of time to argue with an owner determined to stick it out. There are lots of other properties out there waiting to be picked up for a song and a dance.

The Transfer of Property

After you and the homeowner agree to terms, all he needs to do is sign over the deed to the property to you and you pay him. Keep in mind, the sooner you complete this transaction the better. You need to be aware of the date at which it is too late to cure the loan. This information you should have received earlier from the lender. If you get the deed after this date then the property will still go to the foreclosure sale. Usually you can prevent the property from going to auction if you pay the lender within a week or a few days of the scheduled sale. Ask the lender for the exact date so there are no surprises.

The homeowner must sign a quitclaim deed to convey the property over to you. A quitclaim deed can be obtained from your local office supply store or from your attorney. Your signatures should be notarized so go to a bank and sign the deed in the notary's presence.

Once you have the deed signed and notarized take it to the lender or trustee who is handling the case. Bring with you a cashier's check for the amount needed to cure the loan. At this point they can't do anything about the situation but to accept it. The owner has signed the deed and for all they know has left. You legally own the property and are willing to continue paying on the loan, so its to their best interest to work with you. That's it, the former homeowner is released from a pending foreclosure and you now have a valuable asset.

7

LOANS AND FINANCING

This chapter covers some basic information on refinancing and types of loans which you may obtain or which you may offer buyers who finance directly from you. To make an intelligent decision when refinancing, selling, or negotiating, you'll need to have a basic understanding of real estate financing.

REFINANCING AN EXISTING MORTGAGE

Most lenders refer to the "2-2-2 guidelines" for refinancing. If the homeowner has been in the house for two years, if the interest is at least two points over the current rate, and if he is considering staying in the home for at least two years longer, he ought to consider refinancing.

Typically a homeowner may pay about $2,400 in closing to save $100 a month. At this rate it would take a full two years before the owner would begin to receive the benefits of refinancing.

If it will require more than two years to recoup the closing costs, it is generally not worth it. The shorter the time it takes to make up the amount spent at closing the better. Twelve to eighteen months is considered by many the maximum amount of time to allow. But if the homeowner plans to spend at least 10 or 20 years in the same house, refinancing even a single percentage point lower may be worthwhile.

As an investor, your situation is different. You don't need to rely on the "2-2-2 guideline." You can benefit from refinancing even if you sell almost immediately.

Not every distressed property you find having considerable equity, will also have an assumable mortgage. That doesn't mean it's not worth pursuing. When you purchase the home you will need to get a new loan. You may even decide it best to refinance an already assumable mortgage. This is particularly true if the current interest rate is lower than that on the mortgage.

If you decide not to resell a property immediately but rent it for awhile instead, you can still get the cash from the equity now by refinancing the loan. With this cash you can buy more properties and keep recycling the money you get in equity to acquire more property.

When Tom and Joan Gibson bought their home the interest rate on their 30-year, fixed-rate mortgage was $13^{1}/_{4}$ percent. They put $4,000 down on the new $75,000, three bedroom home in Pennsylvania. Payments on the $71,000 home loan amounted to $799 per month.

Two years later, the interest rate on homes had dropped to such a level that Tom and Joan decided to refinance their mortgage at a lower $9^{5}/_{8}$ percent. The interest rate being as low as it was, Tom took out a loan for $84,000 instead of refinancing on the unpaid balance of the loan. The unpaid balance on his original loan amounted to less then $71,000 which was paid off with the money from the second loan. This left him with $13,000 in ready cash! Four thousand of this went to pay for the refinancing (which included three points); the remaining $9,000 went to pay off other debts such as a car loan and home furnishings.

Despite the fact that they borrowed $13,000 more on their new mortgage, their monthly payments dropped to $706, a savings of $93 a month. Not bad huh? The savings Tom and Joan will experience over the next five years will amount to $5,580! Over the life of the loan, the savings will have amounted to about $33,500.

At first, assuming ownership of a home with a high interest rate mortgage may not sound too enticing. But if there is enough equity in the home, you can refinance it, get some cash and a lower monthly payment. When you rent the home the lower monthly mortgage payment will allow you to earn more from rent.

In a buyers' market interest rates typically decline. If interest rates are lower now than when the home was purchased, a homeowner has many advantages. Tom and Joan lowered their monthly mortgage payments and received a windfall of $13,000 in cash. This new found money was theirs to spend as they pleased. If they wanted, they could have taken a loan out for only the amount needed to pay off the first mortgage. This would have lowered their payments even more. The new payment in this case would be $214 less than the original.

As an investor, refinancing could be an option available to you depending on what you need and want to do with the property. Some investors want to resell property as quickly as possible. Others want to hold onto the property, collect rent, and sell later when real estate has appreciated in value. If you buy property and rent it, you do not get back your investment in the property until you sell it some years in the future. One of the advantages of buying and quickly reselling is getting your investment capital back so you can repeat the process over and over again. Refinancing allows you to receive the cash from the equity immediately, which allows you to recycle it into buying more property and still keep the house as a rental.

If property values are depressed, this may be a very good way to collect real estate. Real estate values quickly rebound following economic recessions. Property may increase in value by as much as 10 percent a year. A home originally valued at $100,000 would be worth $130,000 in three years. This would amount to a $30,000 profit when the home is sold. I've seen this happen following a recession.

CLOSING COSTS

The Cost of Refinancing

One of the big advantages of buying a home with an assumable mortgage is that you avoid most all of the closing costs. If you buy a property which is not assumable or if you refinance a home or take out a new mortgage, however, you must pay closing costs.

You can't expect to get something for nothing, and if you decide to refinance, you're going to have to tangle with the little devils known as closing costs. Like anything else worthwhile in this world, you're going to be forced to spend money to save money. In order to refinance a home, you will be charged what lenders cheerfully call closing or settlement costs, just as a new home buyer would. These fees could run up to two or three thousand dollars. This expense can be taken out of the equity of the home so that you don't actually have to pay anything.

You may wonder why closing costs for refinancing is just about as expensive as when buying a new home. Lenders view refinancing as no different from taking out any new mortgage. In most cases the lender doesn't really know the borrower, and, they argue, it is a completely new loan. When you refinance, in essence, what you are doing is selling your home to yourself. Since you are also the buyer, you are expected to pay all the normal fees charged at closing.

To most homeowners paying these fees seems unfair. After all, they are just rearranging your loan. Even so, before they will process your loan, they must investigate any changes in conditions that may have occurred since you, or in some cases the owner before you, had originally purchased the property.

Refinancing is usually done to take advantage of lower interest rates. For lenders, refinancing is a means to make immediate cash in lieu of the long term payout which the higher interest rate would give. You must factor this cost in your calculations when determining the profit potential of the property. If there is enough equity in the property you can still make a substantial profit.

Discount Points

Everyone in the last couple of decades who has borrowed money to purchase a home has been stuck with paying discount points. But what in blazes are they? What is their purpose? What is a "point" and who gets the discount?

"Discount points" describes a fee the lender charges to adjust the yield on the loan to what market conditions demand. It is often simply expressed in terms of "points" which is one of the most confusing terms used in real estate. The word "point" means one percent of the loan amount. So, for a $60,000 loan, one point would be $600, two points, $1,200, and three points, $1,800. Two, three and four points are typically charged by the lender to adjust the loan.

The charging of points first appeared in the 1970s as a means for lenders to make more money during the first year of the loan. Actually, it is a sneaky way of jacking up the price of the loan without increasing the interest rate. By law there is a legal limit to the rate a lender can charge. By using the point system, lenders are getting around this regulation. "Discount points" is a rather elusive term that sounds good, yet doesn't describe anything. Don't be fooled by the term discount; it's no discount to the buyer, only to the lender because he is the one who benefits from it.

The popularity of this concept when it first appeared among lending institutions brings to mind the old wisecrack, "He dashed out of the house, jumped on his horse, and galloped off in all directions." Bankers learning of this new idea acted like the rider—loan discounts spread in all directions so quickly that it wasn't long before all lenders were using them.

Bankers insist that points are used to benefit both the borrower and the lender. They say points can be adjusted to provide the borrower a lower interest rate which saves the home buyer money. As an example, the lender may give the choice of a fixed-rate mortgage at 10 percent with a charge of three points or at $10^1/2\%$ with only one point to pay. This allows the buyers, according to lenders, to choose the terms which suit them best.

Fees and Expenses

In addition to the loan discount, closing costs will include origination fees, appraisal fees, tax search fees, recording fees, legal fees, survey costs, preparation fees, insurance fees, etc. Many of these fees are charged by the lender as another means to stuff more money into his pocket at your expense. Recording fees, preparation fees, insurance fees etc. are charges made to the buyer for filling out a few forms, some of which could just as easily be done by you at a savings of several hundred dollars. Lenders would most likely refuse to let you do it, saying it must be handled by the proper channels. What they mean is it cuts into their profit.

These fees can add up to a substantial amount. In New York, for example, closing costs to refinance a $100,000 mortgage could amount to over $4,000. For some, closing costs could make refinancing uneconomical.

Look at the chart in Appendix C. From this chart you can see how much you will save if you refinance at different rates. If you want to get at the equity in a property you may refinance even if the current interest rate is higher than the mortgage rate. This chart will help you determine what you may pay at different rates.

SHOPPING FOR A MORTGAGE

Reworking the Loan

Several different types of innovative mortgage plans which can drastically lower your monthly payments are available to you. I'm not talking about savings of $50 or $100, but hundreds or even thousands of dollars in some cases. If you're considering refinancing, you have a marvelous opportunity to get a contract with favorable terms.

If you plan on keeping a property for only a couple of years or less, a fixed-rate loan may not be the best for you. You might consider some type of adjustable-rate or balloon loan. You have the opportunity now to change any of the conditions in your loan, including the elimination of any prepayment penalty clause, due-on-sale clause, and the possibility of a deficiency judgment. Negotiate with your lender. He should be willing to bargain with you.

If you are going to refinance an existing loan or get a new loan, don't settle for the first contract that is presented to you. You have a right to make any changes or modifications you want to the contract. Examine the mortgage. Eliminate any and all unfavorable conditions it may contain. You will have to negotiate with the lender in many cases, but it may be well worth your time in the long run.

Don't accept the lender's word or even the word of your lawyer that the contract is okay. The lawyer you hire to check the mortgage agreement will check for obviously illegal or unethical clauses. You may see him for only a few minutes at closing or perhaps not at all. He usually won't point out things like prepayment penalties. You will have to ask him to look for them or read the agreement carefully yourself.

You may also want to consider what's called an open-end mortgage. This allows the homeowner to refinance the home or borrow more money on it at a later date without paying new financing costs. The obvious advantage to this is if you ever want to refinance the home again you won't have to fork over a couple thousand dollars in needless closing costs.

Why would you ever want to refinance again? Who knows what the interest rate is going to be a year from now. Some have predicted rates will drop as low as six percent before they climb to a peak again. Many people who refinanced their loans down to 10 or 11 percent, turned around and refinanced again at 8 percent when rates dropped. Most had to pay the expensive closing costs twice to do this. With an open-end clause in your mortgage, these expenses are eliminated for the most part. Such a clause may make a drop in the market of a single percentage point worthwhile to refinance.

Besides the fluctuating interest rates, who knows what economic conditions will be like in the future? Both lenders and the FHA are devising new mortgage options all the time. You may prefer a new option in a few years, it would be nice if you could slip into it without unnecessary hassles.

Prepayment Penalties

Many people with a prepayment penalty clause in their mortgage suffer with it as they try to refinance. Most of them accepted the prepayment clause as standard practice and paid no attention to it; besides they were buying a home to live in for a long time and didn't plan on moving. Some of these people weren't even aware that their mortgage had a prepayment penalty attached to it.

If your mortgage contains a prepayment clause, it can cost you a pretty penny to refinance. These penalties are added to many loan contracts by the lender to insure him a healthy profit even if the original loan is paid off before reaching maturity. Whether you are refinancing or selling, if you have a prepayment clause you will be required to pay a penalty to the lender when your loan is paid off.

Mortgages with prepayment penalties typically amount to a fee of six month's interest. Refinancing a $60,000, 30-year mortgage can cost anywhere between $4,000 and $5,000 at typical interest rates. This could well be your biggest cost in refinancing and push the total settlement costs to over $6,000! A reduction of monthly payments of $100 in such a case would require a full five years to overcome the initial investment (not including the loss due to the interest the $6,000 would have brought in a savings account or some other investment).

In some states, prepayment penalties are restricted or even prohibited. In the early 1980s when interest rates were at their peak, prepayment penalty clauses in mortgages were common. Many people who are now desiring to refinance are stuck with this nuisance.

If you're working with your original lender, try to negotiate around the prepayment penalty. Some lenders feel it's better to rework the loan rather than lose the business to someone else.

Have Mortgage, Will Travel

Most mortgages do not remain with the original lender for long; they are often put into the secondary market and sold to a third party. At least two thirds of all new mortgages are sold into this secondary market. The buyer could be a bank, finance company, insurance company or other firm and even an investor. The original lender makes a commission on the sale, and if he continues to handle the operation of the mortgage, he is paid a regular servicing fee from the new mortgage holder. In some cases, the homeowner will be instructed to send all mortgage payments to another company altogether.

If your mortgage has been passed to a third party, contact them instead of your original lender, they may offer you good terms to keep your business.

Refinancing means quick fat profits and many lenders are competing for their share of the market. By all means shop around for the best terms you can get, just as you would with a new home loan. Lenders want your business and they know that if they don't give you a good deal, one of their competitors will.

Choosing A Lender

When refinancing, you are in effect selling and rebuying your own property. The old mortgage is paid off and a new one written. Your original lender is the first person you should consult about a new loan. If he wants to keep your business, he will make some concessions. But since it is a new loan, you don't need to stick with him.

Your first step is to go to your lender and discuss terms of refinancing with him. The lender who currently has the loan, however, in many cases will give you the best deal possible, simply to keep your business. Some lenders offer "modification agreements" to some of their established customers. Rather than shuffling through the paper work required for a typical refinancing and creating a new loan, they will make relatively minor changes on the existing mortgage. This could save the you several hundred dollars in needless closing costs.

Your lender may not require redoing all of the services involved in closing. You can expect to pay for some expenses such as attorney's services, a reappraisal of your property, document preparation and recording fees, origination fees, and of course discount points. Some of the things he may not require is another title search, a new title insurance policy, a credit report, and termite inspection.

Competition has spawned modifications to some of the services associated with closing. For those who are refinancing homes that they have not lived in for long, less costly services can be substituted in some cases. Instead of a full title search, the homeowner can opt for a cheaper "bring to date" title. Also, the existing land survey can be recertified rather than getting a new one. Lenders are dreaming up new ways all the time to entice homeowners so that they can keep our business. When you contact your lender, make it a point to ask if he offers any of these services; if so it could save you a couple hundred dollars.

Just like snowflakes, all lenders are different and so are the terms they will offer. Get on the phone and see what they will do for you. The fact that another lender may offer better terms than your original lender may give you a bargaining chip you can use. If your lender won't budge, take your loan out with another lender with terms that suit you.

Use the phone for your initial contact. Ask to speak to someone about refinancing loans. I have found that those who work for the lenders such as secretaries and clerks, are not the most congenial or friendly people to talk with. Getting accurate information out of them is like squeezing juice out of a turnip, you may get a few drops of liquid but usually wind up with a handful of worthless pulp. Some will be so apathetic that they sound as if you were going to go kick them in the knee, and at times you may feel like doing just that. This attitude is due in part to the swarm of inquires they receive from people like yourself who are trying to refinance and are, in their opinion, asking silly questions. In many cases they are just too busy to care about public relations. People will always need loans to buy homes so lenders will always have customers.

Remember, when dealing with these people, you are the customer. You will be paying a lot of money to them. It's people like you that keep them in business. After all, lenders are in the business of lending money, and if they don't have any borrowers then they don't make any money.

LENDING RESOURCES

Who lends money to home buyers? Banks and savings and loans aren't the only lending institutions. Check out other businesses which lend money to home buyers. They will give you a variety of different options from which to choose. The following is a list and brief discussion of the various types of lenders.

Savings and Loan Associations

Numbering in excess of 4,500 nationwide, savings and loan associations are by far the most important home mortgage source. In some areas of the country, they are the only home financing source available.

In most states they are known as savings and loans associations but in Louisiana they are called homestead associations and in Massachusetts, cooperative banks. Home loans constitute the major part of savings and loan associations business income, and they generally offer terms more favorable than banks.

Commercial Banks

Banks are the second largest source for home loans. Totaling 14,400, they far outnumber savings and loan associations, yet carry less than half as many home mortgages (see graph on page 96). Unlike savings and loan associations, banks generally concentrate on short term investments. The majority of their customers are businesses with loans ranging from 6 months to 3 years. Banks do supply home loans but in such cases prefer short terms, usually 15 years or less.

In rural areas banks are more inclined to offer longer terms because businesses are not as plentiful and they must rely more on home loans for income. Most banks which offer loans extending over 15 years will usually sell them later to another institution and pick up a fee rather than keep the mortgage in their own portfolios.

Mutual Savings Banks

Found primarily in the northeastern United States, mutual savings banks are another major source of home loans. Numbering only about 500, they still carry about six percent of the mortgage market.

Unlike banks and savings and loan associations, the depositors of a mutual savings bank are the owners, and the interest they receive on their investments depends on the bank's success. Like banks, they offer passbook and checking accounts and money market certificates as well as long term home loans. They are charted and controlled by state regulatory agencies in contrast to most banks and savings and loan associations, which are federally charted and regulated.

Mortgage Bankers

After banks and savings and loans associations, the mortgage banker or mortgage company is the next most important source for loans. Mortgage companies specialize in preparing and processing long term home mortgages, then selling them to investors. Those that buy the mortgages are life insurance companies, banks, savings and loan associations, pension or trust funds, and government agencies.

The mortgage company is usually paid by the buyer to service the loan, which involves collecting monthly payments, handling property taxes, insurance and dealing with delinquencies and other problems. In essence, the mortgage banker continues to handle the mortgage as if it still belonged to him. The homeowner may not even be aware that a third party is involved.

If you took out a home loan through a mortgage company, it is most likely now owned by another institution. Commercial banks, savings and loan associations, and mutual savings banks also sell mortgages to a lesser extent.

Mortgage Brokers

In contrast to mortgage bankers and other lenders, mortgage brokers do not lend money, nor do they service loans. Their function is much the same as the real estate agent who brings buyer and seller together. Their purpose is to find the home buyer a lender who will provide a loan at the most economical terms available. The borrower then works with the lender to finalize the loan, and the mortgage broker receives a fee, usually expressed in points, as a reward for his services.

HOME MORTGAGE LENDERS

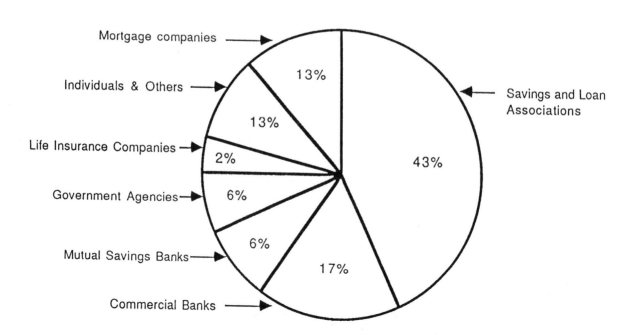

In most cases, you would be better off not using a mortgage broker. You can save yourself the broker's fee by finding you own lender.

Life Insurance Companies

Insurance companies have been active in real estate for a long time and have a major influence on the business. Even though only about two percent of all home loans are obtained from them, they are a major mortgage buyer on the secondary market. The mortgage you originally had from your local bank may now be owned by an out of state insurance company.

There are 1,800 life insurance companies in the United States, all of which are actively involved in real estate investments. Home mortgages actually provide their financial backbone.

Government Agencies

The federal government provides loans to some qualified individuals through the Farmers Home Administration (FmHA) which makes loans available to farmers and other rural dwellers, and the Veterans Administration, which makes loans to veterans if no other financing is available.

Local governments also provide a limited number of loans to finance home mortgages. Some cities will issue municipal bonds to raise money for this purpose. Those who qualify for these loans typically will pay three percent less than they would with commercial lenders. These loans, however, are targeted for lower and middle income home buyers. Usually the housing must be located in predetermined neighborhoods, often as a means to revitalize an area.

I've included this source because you may run across it in your real estate transactions, But for your purposes, loans through this source wouldn't be worth your time pursuing.

Finance Companies

Lending is a finance company's business, and many of them specialize in home financing. Generally, finance companies seek mortgages which are two to five percent higher than the prevailing interest rates; therefore, second mortgages make up the bulk of their mortgage portfolio.

Credit Unions

Traditionally credit unions have specialized in smaller short term loans. Recently they have been branching out into the real estate market. With many of the 23,000 credit unions now offering to finance home mortgages, this could be an excellent source to investigate.

Individuals

Private investors, home sellers, friends, and family are another source for home mortgages. Usually terms are short, 10-15 years or less, and often interest rates are lower and closing costs minimal. In most cases going to a private lender is the most economical way to get financing.

Seller financing is an excellent way for you to sell property and receive a monthly payment. This concept was discussed in some detail in the last chapter.

TYPES OF LOANS

In this section some of the most common types of loans are discussed, including the standard government insured loans and conventional loans. When looking for financing, you should consider all aspects of the loan and shop around, investigating different types of mortgage options. The fixed-rate mortgage has been a standard, but others are also available. Don't jump into any one just because that's what most home buyers get. There are other options available to you that may be much more profitable.

Knowing about the different types of loans will help you whether you are interested in refinancing a loan for a property you already own or whether you are looking for the best type of loan to offer to those who finance from you.

I have included here the most popular forms of financing. These are by no means all that are available, but these have been around for a while or will be around for some time. You won't have an interest in getting involved in all the loan options listed below, but these are the types of loans you will run into as you buy and sell property.

Government Insured Loans

Federal Housing Administration. The FHA is the primary source for government insured loans. They do not actually lend money, as some believe, but guarantee the lender against loss if the borrower defaults.

Before 1957 all insured mortgages were either FHA or VA backed. Since then, MGIC and other private insurance companies have come on the scene and have taken a huge share of the insurance market. Presently one out of every five mortgages is FHA insured.

There are some distinct benefits to having a FHA backed loan. You can buy property with a down payment under five percent. You're also allowed to borrow all your closing costs, which further reduces your need for cash. How large an FHA loan you can get depends on where you live. In certain high-cost housing areas, you'll be able to borrow up to $197,621. This maximum loan is available to buyers earning $65,380 and up. It supports a home costing as much as $203,000. With a smaller income, you'll have to shop for a cheaper home. In lower-cost areas, you'll be able to borrow up to $109,032. There, you'll qualify for the maximum loan with an income of $38,270 and up and you can buy a house for as much as $115,000.

The FHA accepts people with fewer assets than banks normally require, and less-than-ideal credit profiles. Prepayment penalties are not allowed with any government guaranteed loan, something that may be of importance to you later. These homes are also easier to sell because they are assumable, while most conventional loans are not.

Another attraction that government backed loans have had, and to some extent still do, are lower interest rates. Because the loans were insured, they were considered safer for the lender who could, in turn, offer a slightly lower rate. The FHA also screens each applicant to assure they are financially stable enough to make the payments.

In times past, the FHA has set a maximum interest rate which is usually one half to one percent less than conventional loans; a potentially significant saving. One percent interest on a $70,000 loan for thirty years would amount to about $19,000.

The government no longer sets the interest rate on its loans. Rates are now determined by the current market, but they are often still lower than conventional loans. Like conventional loans, there is now no limit on the number of points that can be charged. You are going to have to shop around for an FHA backed loan just as you would a conventional one.

FHA loans are generally a good deal, especially for new home buyers with little cash. The government has purposely designed and regulated FHA loans to help homeowners who otherwise wouldn't be able to qualify for a loan. Since these loans are meant to help the homeowner, they are restricted to that purpose. FHA insured mortgages are available only for homes purchased as the primary residence of the home buyer. Real estate investors who buy two or more homes must obtain conventional loans. The only way an investor can get an FHA or VA loan is to buy the property from the original owner on assumption. As you've seen in previous chapters this is an excellent way to obtain investment property. You can, then turn around and resell the property to another person who, like you, assumes the original mortgage.

All home buyers who go the FHA route will need to have the down payment and closing costs in hand at time of settlement. The borrower is not allowed to take out a loan such as a second mortgage in order to get money for the down payment. This regulation is of more concern to someone who is buying a new home than it is for someone who is refinancing.

One of the biggest drawbacks with government insured loans is the bureaucratic red tape and extra paper work required to process the loan. Because of this, not all lenders offer FHA loans. You can expect an additional three to five weeks waiting for an FHA loan. The people at the FHA, however, are continually trying to improve their loan approval methods and are gradually speeding up the approval process.

Veterans Administration. In order to show its appreciation to servicemen who fought in World War II, Congress in the 1940's passed legislation which provided veterans many benefits. One of the organizations created was the Veterans Administration whose purpose was to assist veterans in buying homes.

The original GI Bill of 1944 was limited only to WWII veterans but has since been extended to include all veterans who have served at least 180 days and been honorably discharged.

Like the FHA, the Veterans Administration provides lenders with a guarantee that the government will pay off part of the loan if the borrower defaults. Applicants must satisfy certain requirements to determine if they will be able to pay back the loan. Since its inception, over 9 million homes have been obtained through the help of the Veterans Administration.

VA insured loans generally have the same advantages and disadvantages as FHA loans with a few noticeable differences. The VA requires an even lower down payment than the FHA and does not charge an insurance fee. For VA loans, the lender is insured 100% for the first $25,000 and 95% for the remainder. Many veterans have been able to move into a new home with absolutely no down payment, which is one of its major advantages.

Unlike FHA loans, the loan discounts are still limited to only one point, providing those who qualify the opportunity to purchase a home for a minimum initial cost.

Policies concerning VA loans are continually changing. For further information call your local HUD or VA office listed in the phone book under United States Government. In Appendix B of this book, I have included a listing of all HUD offices in the United States. Find the one closest to you and give them a call.

Conventional Loans

Simply stated, a conventional mortgage is one that is not government guaranteed. They are either privately insured or carry no insurance at all. Most home loans are of this type.

Policies governing conventional loans are as numerous as the lenders themselves. Within certain government regulations, lenders are free to structure their loaning practices as they see fit, setting their own qualifications and terms. The policies governing FHA loans have been looked at as a standard and most conventional loans follow suit.

Traditionally, the fixed-rate mortgage has been the most preferred type of loan. The borrower can lock into a preset interest rate for the life of the loan without the worry of payments increasing, except when taxes go up.

The types of loans permitted by the FHA and VA are limited to a very few. Conventional loans, on the other hand, have no limit and the number and variety of terms is continually changing. In the following section we will look at some of these loans and how to choose the one most suited for you.

Adjustable-Rate Mortgages

In the early 1980s as interest rates began to shoot through the ceiling, lenders, stuck with a multitude of older low interest loans, wracked their brains to figure out ways to increase their profits. The idea that came to mind was the adjustable interest rate mortgage. This new mortgage was gradually adapted by all types of lenders as the answer to climbing interest rates. In contrast with the fixed-rate mortgage, interest rates on the adjustable-rate "float" with the market, giving lenders a continual cushion of profit.

No buyer in his right mind would take such a mortgage in a time of rising inflation, so in order to entice borrowers to accept these terms, the initial interest rate was set at one, two, or even three points below the prevailing rate. As interest rates continued to climb, more and more people found it difficult to qualify for home loans. The new adjustable-rate mortgage (ARM's) made it possible for many of these people to get loans because they could qualify at the lower interest rate.

When they were introduced, ARM's sky-rocketed into popularity, so much so that articles published in 1980 were predicting the end of the fixed-rate mortgage. By August of 1984 ARM's accounted for over 68% of all new mortgages.

When interest rates began to fall, however, so did the appeal for ARM's. By May of 1986, only 27% of the new mortgages were of this type and the percentage has continued to drop. Many who have ARM's are now refinancing them in exchange for more reliable fixed-rate mortgages. Some analysts have predicted that the ARM will eventually die (at least for the present). Many lenders, however, are working hard to keep them alive. In order to persuade new home buyers to take an ARM, lenders are using all their powers of creative financing. They are adding sweeteners to this mortgage in hopes of attracting customers even in the face of already low interest rates. Although still not nearly so popular as they once were, I believe they are here to stay.

Why did ARM's rise to such popularity only to tumble to near oblivion in only a few short years? The major attraction was the initial lower interest rate. In the first half of 1984 an ARM could be obtained for $11^1/2\%$ while fixed-rate mortgages were going for 13%.

The rate at the start of the loan could be as much as three points lower than other types of loans. This feature drew many into its grasp. The stickler that eventually led to its unpopularity was the floating interest rate. When interest rates went up, so did the payments. Many people with ARM's who had enjoyed the downward slide in rates below 9% have traded them in on fixed-rate loans to lock into some stability.

One of the major reasons ARM's lost much of their appeal is that the spread between them and fixed-rate mortgages shrunk to about one percentage point, hardly enough to take the risk.

As bleak as it may sound, ARM's are still alive and apparently will remain so for some time. Adjustable-rate mortgages are a lender's dream, and because lenders hate to see them fade into obscurity, some lenders are putting sweeteners in their ARM's to attract new customers. A few institutions are clinging desperately to them and financing almost nothing but. Great Western Financial Corporation of California, for example, has built a portfolio consisting of 80% ARM's. The interest rate has been lowered two or more percentage points below other mortgages and charging as little as 1.5 points. Apparently customers are biting, and other lenders are following suit.

There is no legal limit as to how far or how often the interest rate can move. The rate is tied to one of any number of publicly available indexes: yields on Treasury bills, or the average cost of funds to savings and loans which is published by the Federal Home Loan Bank Board. The borrower should be aware of which one is used. Make sure the rate can decrease as well as increase. If the rates go down, you don't want to be stuck with an index that doesn't. Linking into a Treasury bill would be more advantageous then the bank's cost funds. That is because the cost funds index could actually be rising while other rates are going down.

Changes in the interest rate can be accommodated for in three ways. The first and most obvious is adjusting the monthly mortgage payments. The other two methods rely on changing the term of the loan or the principal owed.

Adjustable monthly payment is the simplest solution to fluctuating interest rates. If rates change, the payments are adjusted to the new rate. If rates increase, so do monthly payments. This can be scary if interest rates sky rocket as they did in the early 1980s.

A $720 payment can swell to $950 on a $70,000 home with a rise of just three percent. Such a rapid rise in payments could be devastating to a budget. A sudden rise of $200 or more could well put someone into a financial bind.

Having this happen can be a frightful experience, causing many to seek other forms of financing.

To relieve this fear, two other means of accommodating changes in interest rates have been used. In both methods the monthly payments remain constant, giving some degree of stability. If the payments remain constant, something else of value must then change to accommodate for a floating interest. One or these ways is to adjust the term of the loan. If rates decrease, than the length of your mortgage will shorten. If, however, rates rise, the term of the loan will increase. A 30-year loan can swell into a 35 or 40-year loan with the same monthly payment.

If an adjustable term doesn't appeal to you, the second option would be to adjust the principal. If rates go down, the principal you are required to pay goes down. If the rate goes up, your principal goes up. Conceivably you can get into a hairy situation with this. If rates continue to rise and remain at an elevated level, you could end up owing more money when the mortgage matures in twenty years than you originally borrowed. You make regular payments but the amount you owe increases. This is called negative amortization and is a nasty thing to get tied into.

For many, neither of these two options is any more desirable than the first. To ease the fears of borrowers and make ARM's more enticing, limits can be written into the agreements.

Since nobody knows how high rates can or will climb over the life of a loan, a ceiling can be set. If the loan starts out at 10 percent, the absolute highest that can be required may be set at 15 percent, regardless of how high the national index goes. A five percent difference is the maximum you should allow, less if possible.

Another concern is if rates rise too rapidly, payments can jump two or three hundred dollars in a matter of months. To help ease fears, limits on the rate of change can also be put into the agreement. This limit may be 2% (3% or whatever) a year. No matter what the index does, the rate the homeowner will pay can only change by a specified amount annually.

Changes in rates can fluctuate rapidly. Nobody would like the thought of a payment plan that changed every month. A minimum interval is used to provide some stability. Rate changes at intervals of six months are the minimum. Usually, the interval is set on a yearly basis but can change every two, three, or five years.

You must ask that each of these special conditions be written into your agreement. Don't expect your lender to automatically give you the best terms, he wants to make as much money as he can.

Even with these added sweeteners nowadays, ARM's are a tough sell to most home buyers. With interest rates as low as they are, people are choosing to lock into some stability rather than take a risk with the rates exploding again. With the initial savings down to about one percent the risk just doesn't seem worth it.

For an investor who plans on reselling the property quickly an ARM is very enticing. He can get an initial interest rate two or perhaps three percentage points below the fixed-rate mortgages and thus lower his monthly mortgage payments to bare minimum. Since the property is soon sold you wouldn't have to worry about the rates rising in the future. So you enjoy the benefit of significantly lower mortgage rates as you market the property.

If you think an ARM is what you want, shop around. A number of different arrangements can be worked out. Some lenders will give a lower interest rate with a higher lifetime cap or lower the cap but increase the initial rate. It's even possible to get a clause which will allow you to switch to a fixed-rate loan at low cost. So, you can work out almost any type of arrangement that would work best for you. For an investor who wants to resell the property within a year or two your goal would be to lower the initial interest rate as much as possible. You can agree to things that won't affect you much as a compromise, such as a higher cap or increasing length of loan from 30 to 40 years. You may adjust the interest rates to reduce or even eliminate closing costs and still end up with rates lower than the standard fixed-rate loans.

In the past, the government has restricted itself to fixed-rate loans. With the increased popularity of the ARM in the early 80s, the FHA has been authorized to insure these loans as well. The terms under the direction of the FHA are fairly standard and probably some of the best available. As of this writing the terms for FHA insured ARM's are: 1) five percent maximum allowable ceiling rate over the life of the loan, 2) annual interest rate adjustments with a maximum increase of one percent, 3) no negative amortization. As you buy assumable FHA loans you may run across some ARMs.

Graduated Payment Mortgage

This innovative mortgage was created by the Department of Housing and Urban Development to help young couples just starting out and others who expect to have a gradual increase of income. It is offered by the FHA, VA, and a few private lenders.

With a graduated payment mortgage (GPM) the length of the loan and the interest rate are fixed but the monthly payments vary. In this way, a borrower with a low initial income who has potential for continued increase can start with relatively low payments. As time progresses and as earning power increases, payments are increased.

As an example, an 11 percent, 30-year loan on $70,000 would require monthly payments of $667 at a fixed-rate. With a GPM, the payments may start out at $577 then gradually increase to $705 after the tenth year. It would then remain at this level for the rest of the term of the loan.

The homeowner pays less initially and more each year until reaching a specified date, usually five or ten years. Since the interest rate remains constant the latter payments must compensate for the early low payments, but the overall expense to the homeowner is the same as that of a fixed-rate loan.

A GPM can be an attractive mortgage plan to first-time home buyers and especially to investors. Whether you are buying property to turn around and resell quickly or to hang on to as a rental a GPM could work well for you.

If you plan to resell the property as quickly as possible it is a good mortgage to have because you never know how long you are going to keep the property until it sells. While you own it, you must continue to make mortgage payments. It's to your advantage to have the lowest payments possible to reduce your expenses. Even if the home sells within a month you save. This savings may be $100 or more. If the home doesn't sell for two or three months the savings can become very significant. If you've been able to eliminate the due-on-sale clause so that the mortgage is assumable, then it is an enticement to potential buyers because they see the monthly payments as lower than comparable properties. You are not as concerned with the interest rate as you are the mortgage payments for the first year or so. You will resell the property long before the rates increase and benefit from the reduced rates. Buyers also will look at the low mortgage payments as an incentive to buy.

If you plan to rent the property a GPM is also inviting. You will only keep the rental property four, five or six years. During that time you can be paying a lower mortgage rate than normal. You will sell the property long before the rate escalates. By this time the property will have appreciated in value and you will have gotten a higher rate of return from rent as well as the equity.

Balloon Mortgages

The name for this type of mortgage is aptly chosen. It can start out small but quickly swell to large proportions. For a homeowner who isn't careful, it could very well "explode" with a great financial consequences.

A balloon mortgage essentially is one in which the final payment is substantially larger then any of the previous ones. Monthly payments start off very low and on a specified date, 5, 10, 15 years later, the balance of the loan becomes due in full.

This is an innovative way to go if you want your payments to be at a rock bottom level and are confident that you will either sell the property before maturity or have accumulated enough money to make the final payment when it's due. In the past, many balloon mortgages have "popped" on the borrower and property repossessed. The final payment date creeping up and throwing the homeowner into a bind.

A balloon mortgage provides an opportunity to get the lowest payments possible, usually amounting to just the interest. This type of loan provides investors with another excellent opportunity to finance a mortgage with the smallest initial monthly payments possible. Long before the loan comes due you have sold the property and never have to worry about it.

Many investors have purchased property with a balloon mortgage and wait for housing prices to rise again. In most cases this strategy will work especially if the property was purchased in a depressed market at a discount. The house could be sold in a healthier market before the mortgage becomes due. Sounds attractive, but before committing to this type of loan and this type of strategy make sure you understand all of the terms and what will be required on the final payment.

Roll-Overs

Roll-overs are an outgrowth of the balloon mortgage and are a much more reasonable type of loan. Payments are made at a fixed-rate that would normally amortize the loan at 30 years or so. The difference is that the due date for the final balloon payment is much sooner, usually three, five, or seven years.

The added feature that distinguishes this loan from an ordinary balloon mortgage is the option to roll over the loan into a fixed-rate mortgage at the time the final payment is due. This feature acts as a built in safety valve so that homeowners who aren't able to make the final payoff still have a way out. The loan is renewed at the current interest rate for 15 to 30 years allowing the borrower to refinance without the hassle and much of the expense of closing costs.

Roll-overs are definitely more risky than an ordinary fixed-rate loan but safer then the standard balloon mortgage. This type of mortgage is most popular with those who don't plan on keeping the property for the full duration for the loan. Unfortunately, not everyone can predict what will happen to them five or seven years down the road. Because of unforeseen circumstances the owner may be stuck with the house when the loan matures. Having the option to renew the mortgage with different terms is a relief.

You may want to think seriously about this type of mortgage. The assurance that you can always roll over to a fixed-rate will ease your mind in the mean time.

Growing Equity Mortgage

The growing equity mortgage (GEM) is another mortgage plan that starts out with low payments and builds with time. GEM's are fixed-rate mortgages. The interest rate remains constant but payments increase by about three percent each year until the loan is paid off, which is usually about 15 years. Many banks as well as other lenders are willing to offer an interest rate below the current one for GEM's because the loan is paid off sooner.

In the early stages of most mortgages, almost all of the money you put into your payments goes just to pay off the interest. Only a measly portion is extracted to reduce the principal. As interest is paid off, you begin to put more money towards reducing the principal and increasing your equity. For example, on a 30-year mortgage at 10 percent, after ten years of payments a homeowner will still owe 90 percent of the principal amount.

With a GEM the increase in payments each year goes toward paying off the principal. Since you pay interest on only the principal, the smaller the principal you have, the quicker you will be able to pay off the loan. You are actually paying off the principal sooner, decreasing the total amount of interest you would otherwise pay.

Let me throw some figures together to give you an idea what payments would be like. Monthly payments which start out at $600 can grow with a three percent increase each year to $908 by the 15th year.

Shared Appreciation Mortgage

Known as SAM, this mortgage option has not been popular with many home buyers. It's best suited to economic climates in which interest rates are high, although it may be offered to financially troubled homeowners who are trying to refinance.

The name shared appreciation is descriptive. The borrower gives the lender a portion of the property's appreciation in return for a lower rate of interest. When the house is sold, the lender then is entitled to a percentage of the equity, normally in the range of 30 to 50 percent.

In some cases, the buyer is required to sell the home at a specified time. If the homeowner does not sell by this date, he is liable for the appraised amount of the lender's share. To put it bluntly, this is a lousy situation to get into.

In order to entice prospective buyers, a lender instead of charging the going rate of say 12%, would drop it to 8% in exchange for a third or more of the appraised value of the property. To me this is like dangling bait on a fishing line. The homeowner taking the bait may wind up in the fryer.

In 1980 when interest rates were blasting skyward, many people jumped at the chance to get a home at greatly reduced levels through this type of mortgage. In August of that year, one Florida savings and loan offered SAM's at a rate of 5% while the current market value was hanging over 12 percent. Their take was one-third of the appreciation of the property when it was sold or refinanced. Such a low interest rate drew a tremendous response and, after only one day, the savings and loan had given their limit of $2^1/_2$ million.

Obviously, when interest rates are high, SAM's become more inviting.

The lender may set a limit, say 10 or 15 years, on the loan after which the owner must sell and split the profits accordingly. If the homeowner does not want to sell, he must pay the lender his share of the appreciation.

Assuming a 6% appreciation for ten years, a $70,000 house financed with a SAM would have increased in value to $118,260. The amount owed to the lender would be $16,087 plus the remaining balance on the loan, a hefty sum to pay all at once if the owner decides he doesn't want to sell.

Shared Equity Mortgage

Shared equity mortgages, also known as partnership mortgages, are just that—a sharing in the ownership of the property. The mortgage loan itself can be most any type, such as a fixed-rate, but the down payment, closing costs, or even some of the payments are paid by a third party in exchange for a share of the equity in the property. This third party can be anyone who does not live in the house with the primary owner.

Parents and relatives have been providing financial assistance like this for many years. When this type of mortgage first came out it was considered by the IRS to be either a gift or a personal loan. Since then shared equity mortgages can be treated as investments. Being a investment the third party, whether a relative or not, can enjoy certain tax advantages.

For someone who doesn't have the ready cash to refinance, a friend, relative, or investor can provide the money as an investment. The homeowner then can repay with a monthly rent payment to the investor or share a percentage of the profits when the house is sold. All this should be worked out before financing is completed.

Reverse Account Mortgage

More applicable to buying a new house than to refinancing, this method has shown promise of becoming one of the more popular forms of financing. A reverse account mortgage is a creative type of financing that is aimed at helping buyers purchase a home for little or no money down.

In exchange for lenient down payment terms, the borrower arranges for a deposit to be made into an interest-bearing account with the lending institution that is providing the loan. This deposit which can vary, but may be about 5% of the property value, can be deposited by anyone: a friend, the builder, a real estate agent, or anybody else.

The money remains in the account for a specific number of years (usually two or three) and serves as a type of temporary equity. If the homeowner defaults on the loan, the money becomes the property of the lender and is used to cover the costs of foreclosure.

If the homeowner makes all scheduled payments, after a predetermined time the account with interest reverts back to the depositor.

Having this account provides the lender some security until the buyer begins to build equity and personal attachment to the new home.

Besides the lenient down payment terms, private mortgage insurance is not required, amounting to an additional savings. Current interest rates are used so there is no compromise in this respect. The only drawback is a fee charged by the lender which amounts to about one percent of the loan and is added into the closing costs fee.

8

CASHING IN ON YOUR INVESTMENTS

SELLING VS RENTING

Once you start to acquire real estate, you need to decide whether to keep it as rental property, or sell it for a quick profit. If you keep the property and rent it out, you can gain enough from rent to pay the mortgage and incidental maintenance costs and perhaps even earn a small profit each month. The big advantage to retaining ownership to the property is that as time passes the property will increase in value so that when you do sell, you will receive a bigger return on your investment.

The obvious drawback with renting is that you must wait until you sell the property before you can cash in on your investment. Another thing to consider is your time and energy spent at managing the rental property—getting renters, dealing with problems, periodic maintenance, and such. Although this doesn't take a lot of time, it is something to consider.

If the housing market is soft, and property isn't selling quickly, investors typically rent their houses until the market picks up. Everyone is in need of housing and you will find someone to rent regardless of the economy. However, later in this chapter I will show you how to find eager buyers even in the most depressed economy.

If the housing market is soft, many investors will keep their properties as rentals until real estate values increase. Even in a depressed economy when property values may be dropping, if you wait long enough the market will turn around. Real estate is the best investment anyone can make because property values, on average, always go up—they always have and always will. There is a limited amount of real estate available for a growing population seeking the American Dream of home ownership. Although there has been minor dips in value during severe economic times, property values have always rebounded and soared higher than ever before. If you buy a property at market value for $80,000 and the next year values drop so that your home is only worth $75,000 will you lose money? Well, you will if you try to sell it at market value. But if you hold on it for a few years, its value will rebound higher than the $80,000 you paid and may appreciate very significantly. Renting has always been considered a means by which investors can hold on to property while they wait for values to rebound.

If you can sell your property quickly, without having to rent it, you get a faster return on your investment. However, most investors see homes as a long term investment. They buy a home for say $80,000 and hold onto it for 10, 15, 20 years, waiting for property values to increase, as they always do over the long run. Then they sell at the current market value, which by then may have increased to $140,000. They reap a $60,000 profit. Not bad. It's easy to see why people do this. This is one reason why home ownership is so enticing, you can always count on the home you're living in to increase in value. The only drawback is that you have to hold on to the property for many, many years in order to see this type of profit.

But there is a smarter way. If you bought the same home for $80,000 and turned around and resold it in a few weeks for $90,000, you would have a $10,000 profit almost immediately. If you did this again every couple of months, you could easily be making $40,000 to $60,000 a year. At this rate, rather than waiting 10 or 20 years to earn $60,000, as in the case with the above example, you could earn the same amount after only one year! Just think how much you could earn in 10 or 20 years. You don't need to go after huge profits with each transaction. There is actually more profit potential in buying and selling many properties for smaller amounts.

By investing in select foreclosed and distressed properties you are guaranteeing yourself a sizable profit with each sale, and with the techniques discussed below you will be able to sell that property, regardless of the current economic climate, for a substantial profit.

HOW TO BE A GOOD FSBO

If you are going to make any money in real estate you need to learn how to market and sell the properties yourself. Property sold without the aid of a real estate agent is called a FSBO or "For Sale By Owner". Using a real estate agent to help you sell your property and paying his or her commission will seriously erode your profit. If you're going to learn how buy property, you should also learn how to sell it. These are part of the skills you will develop as a real estate investor.

Consider the cost of using the services of an agent. If you sold a house for $150,000 and your equity in the property was $20,000, a commission of 6% would amount to $9,000 or nearly half of your equity. If you only had $15,000 in equity the commission would be a whopping 60% of your equity. The commission will eat away your entire profit.

If you are just starting out in real estate investment you might ask: "Won't the skills and expertise of a real estate agent be worth the expense, at least in the beginning, until I become more familiar with the business?" The answer is "no." The reason is because Realtors market and sell all their client's properties in the same way and rely on the buyer getting a commercial loan to finance the sale. It's through creative financing, however, that you will sell most of your property and gain your biggest profits. Agents don't really understand real estate financing and, therefore, would be of little help to you.

Do your homework and keep the profit, you've earned it. If you need help with contracts or other real estate matters, use a lawyer. An attorney would be cheaper anyway. Your expense for legal services will be a few hundred dollars as compared to several thousand on an agent's commission. Once you become more familiar with the laws and procedures of real estate investing you will have less need for legal counsel.

Look for a lawyer who is familiar with real estate. At your first meeting, tell your lawyer that you are selling your home without a broker and expect him to draw the contract, deed, and other necessary documents and also handle the title closing. Ask him what his fee will be to represent you throughout the transaction. It's common to charge a fee equal to $1/2$ to 1 percent of the sale price.

Enhance the Value of Your Property

One of the very first things you should do once you've acquired a house is to prepare it for sale. Most homes that are headed toward or go into foreclosure need work. Owners facing the possibility of losing their homes stop spending time and money keeping the property up. It will need yard work and perhaps some repairs. Get started on this at once.

A little investment in cleaning up the property can make a big difference in the selling price and in the length of time it stays on the market. One of the big motivating factors for home buyers in selecting a house is its appearance. If it looks appealing half the battle is won. Likewise, a charming house can look unappealing if it us unkempt.

Do everything you can that will enhance the appearance of the property without wasting money on things that won't make much of a difference.

The first thing you should do and also the cheapest is to remove trash, cut the lawn, trim hedges, pull weeds and such. Make the yard look as clean and trim as possible.

Clean the inside of the house as well, especially the bathrooms and kitchen. Make the house as odor-free as possible. Odor can be a real turn-off.

Fix or replace all the little things like torn screens, broken light fixtures, missing or burnt-out light bulbs, light switches and outlet plates covered heavily with paint, leaky or broken faucets, doorknobs that don't work, and the like. These are little things that a new owner doesn't want to be bothered with and it shows the house was well kept, suggesting that everything else in the home received similar care.

Once you've finished the facelift, you may consider more expensive items. Fix any serious problem like a leaky roof or dripping water pipe. No one wants a home that has water problems. Just painting over water stains isn't enough if the leak persists because this can be interpreted as hiding a fault from the buyer and can cause you legal problems. Clean the carpet. Have it patched if necessary. Clean carpet and flooring can be a real selling feature to a prospective buyer. Make the property look as nice as possible with the least expense.

What you should not do is pour money into the home that won't enhance it salability by much. A new coat of paint will make the house more attractive, but the expense may not be worth it. An old furnace may look old but replacing it will not change the value of the home. As long as it's working, leave it alone or have it serviced. Don't replace anything that doesn't need replacing. Don't upgrade the home by adding storm windows, doing landscaping, wallpapering or redecorating, as the cost will not be justified. You may spend $2,000 landscaping, but only increase the value by $500. Paint, wallpaper, and such are personal preferences and might not appeal to new owners.

If a $70,000 home could use $10,000 in repairs to make it worth $82,000, leave that job to a buyer who is willing to do the repairs. Many people who have the skills, or access to those with the skills, will jump at the opportunity to buy the house and do the repairs to get a "good" deal. Let them have it.

Asking Price

The secret to doing this is being able to resell quickly. The longer you hold onto a property, without renters, the more money you will end up paying in mortgage and the less profit you will receive. If you turned around and tried to resell for full market value, it may take several months before it sold. This is far too long. To guarantee a quick sale you should consider asking a price that is below the market value. This way both investors and new home buyers will feel they are getting a great deal—a deal too good to pass up. Sure you forfeit the possibly of getting a few thousand more dollars, but if the house doesn't sell for six months, you may end up paying more in mortgage payments than you would have given up in the beginning and you would have wasted lots of time in trying to sell the property, time you could have spent finding more foreclosures and earning more money.

Let's say you find a home which you calculate to have about $20,000 in equity. The property has a loan balance of $90,000. It is in a good neighborhood and comparable to homes selling for $110,000 or more. The amount needed to pay for back payments, fees and other expenses may amount to $5,000.

You figure you can resell the home for $110,000—your estimate of fair market value. But you want a quick sale. At fair market value the property may sit vacant for several months before it eventually sells. Therefore, you want to make the property enticing to other investors and potential homeowners and offer them a deal they can't pass up. Plan on reselling at $103,000. This gives investors room to make a profit if they buy it or a family to jump at the bargain. The philosophy you should keep in mind for quick sales is "pigs get fat, hogs get slaughtered." Every month the home doesn't sell you will have to make mortgage payments. This can eat a big hole into your profit and may erode it entirely if the home doesn't sell for awhile. It's best to offer a good deal and sell quickly.

Your potential return would be $12,000—the difference between the loan amount ($90,000) and the projected selling price ($102,000). You must decide what your time and effort is worth to you.

ADVERTISING

Yard Sign

From day one, you should have a sign up in the yard advertising it for sale. Don't worry about not having it completely fixed up yet, get that sign up working for you as soon as possible. If no one knows the home is for sale it's not going to be sold, so begin your marketing from the start by putting up that sign.

Buy a nice looking sign that's comparable in quality to the ones real estate agents use. You can get one from a sign company. It doesn't need to be expensive, just so it doesn't look like a cheap garage sale sign. The words "For Sale" and the phone number should be large. Special features like a "pool" may also be listed. You may use "3-2-2" to indicate number of bedrooms (3), bathrooms (2), and size of garage (two-car). Be careful not to put so much on the sign as to clutter it up. Generally, the simpler the sign, the better. See example below:

```
+-------------------------+     +-------------------------+
|       FOR SALE          |     |       FOR SALE          |
|       by Owner          |     |       by Owner          |
|  Shown by appointment   |     |         3-2-2           |
|       555-1234          |     |      Call 555-1234      |
+-------------------------+     +-------------------------+
```

A good way to attract those buyers who are the most receptive is to use a brochure box attached to the sign. The brochure box is a small mail box which can hold a one-page description of the home. This brochure is often called a "listing sheet." The small mail boxes to hold these sheets can be obtained at most any hardware or lawn and garden store. The listing sheet is a standard sized piece of white paper, $8^1/2$ x 11-inches, providing all pertinent information on the property such as address of the home, asking price, size, number of bedrooms, and, of course, your name and phone number. You might also list special selling features such as name of local schools, large fireplace, on cul-de-sac, hot tub, quiet neighborhood, and the like.

You can find many of the specifications about the property for the listing sheet from documents you obtained when you bought the property.

A photograph of the front of the home should also be included on this information sheet. You can take a picture with any camera. In the photo, include the entire house and as much of the landscaping and trees as possible. Try to get an angle view to show the depth of the house and lot. Wait for a bright, sunny day to get a clear photo. Make sure the house is free from signs, cars, ladders, or other equipment that would distract from your house and yard. Make certain the lawn is freshly cut and trimmed and all visible exterior repairs have been completed before you take these photos. Remember, what the buyer sees is what the buyer assumes he is getting. Take several shots and choose the best photo for your listing sheet.

Attach the photo to the top of your listing sheet and give it to your local quick printer. Have him run a hundred or so copies of the listing on his photocopier. This is cheaper than having it done on a printing press because set up time for presses makes running one or two hundred copies far too expensive. If you took a good picture, the quality of the photocopy will be acceptable. If you have a computer with a scanner, so you can scan in the photo, then you can do it all yourself. This way, you can run off as many as you need. As the saying goes, "a picture is worth a thousand words", this is true. It is an important selling device on your brochure, so don't leave it out.

The listing sheet that you prepare will be an important tool in selling your house. It should be handed out to any and all prospective buyers. You should always prepare these information sheets for each property you sell. The cost is minimal. It is your advertisement for the house. Keep a stack in your car and hand them out like business cards.

Bulletin Boards

Another method of advertising that will not cost you much is bulletin boards. There are bulletin boards in may stores that allow customers to put up card-sized announcements of a variety of things they may be selling, including homes. You might even be able to leave your information sheet as well. These boards are usually cleaned off every week or two so you may want to go back and replace them when necessary.

Word of Mouth

You should let everyone you meet know you are looking to both buy and sell property. Hand out your business card freely. Even if the person you give your card to won't ever need to do business with you, he may pass your card along to someone else who will.

Ask your doctor, the store clerk, auto mechanic, etc. Don't be shy about asking acquaintances if they or anyone they know are selling or looking for a home. You don't need to be obnoxious, just simply state, "I'm selling a home in a great neighborhood, do you know anyone who might be interested?" Or, "I've got a home just around the corner I'm selling, would you know anyone who would be interested?" Believe it or not, you'll find a lot of potential buyers this way.

If one of these people does know someone who might be interested, get their name and phone number if possible, as well as the name of the person giving you the information. When you contact the potential buyer, tell them where you got their name and the name of the person who referred you.

Newspapers

There are several methods businesses use to advertise their products—billboards, magazines, radio and television, newspapers, etc. Most of these are not cost effective for buying or selling real estate. Media advertising is expensive and you should avoid it in most cases. The only exception is newspapers, specifically classified ads.

When people are looking for homes they automatically go to the classified section of the newspaper. This is were homes are advertised. There are two basic types of newspapers that you might consider advertising in, your city newspaper and a shoppers guide. The shoppers guide consists primarily or entirely of advertising and is distributed without cost by local stores. Some cities have several shoppers guides or even small community newspapers. Stick to classified adverting as display ads cost far too much and aren't worth the expense.

Look at the ads in your local paper. Use them as examples. The cost of the ad depends on its size, the longer the ad the more expensive it is. You can save yourself a lot of money if you carefully write your ad to say what needs to be said with the least amount of words. See how others write their ads. Use their ideas, but give only important information that would motivate a potential buyer to give you a call.

The most important information in any real estate ad is location, size, and price. This data should accompany every ad. For most people, these are the three things that they look for when buying a house. They have an idea of the area of town they want to live in or don't want to in. Buyers want to know the size—number of rooms, bathrooms, and garage capacity—because they have certain needs and wants to satisfy. The price is essential because all buyers have a maximum limit they can spend and they will try to get the most for what they can afford. If you don't include the price you will waste your time with people who can't afford the property. Including these three items will attract those prospects who are most likely to buy.

Give the information mentioned above and one or two selling features. That's all. You don't need to describe every feature, you want them to be curious enough to come out and look at the property. See the example below:

> **Stetson Hills**. 3bd, 2ba, 2car, large kitchen, central air, fin basement, many upgrades, mtn view. Beautiful home with lots of charm. $130,000. 555-1234

The basic description in this ad lists the area of town (Stetson Hills), number of bed rooms, bathrooms and garage size, price, and, of course, your phone number. This add includes all the basic information needed as well as providing a couple of selling features.

While this ad is not too bad, it contains information that isn't really necessary and can be just as effective with less cost. "Central air", "finished basement", "many upgrades" are not useful selling points. This house is in located in Colorado where central air is standard for most all homes, making this statement useless. Having a finished basement and many upgrades aren't strong selling features either as the home is expected to be livable and in good condition. A beautiful home with lots of charm is a personal opinion, so let the potential buy decide.

The selling features that are useful in this ad are the "large kitchen" and "mountain view". These statements will attract interest and help distinguish the ad from others.

Examples of some features that aren't particularly effective motivators for most buyers are: custom basement, tri-level or bi-level, vinyl windows, vaulted ceilings, great location, and fenced yard. These may be important features, but they don't make the home stand out above the rest or motive potential buyers to rush to your door anxious to buy.

Amenities that are effective include: cul-de-sac, wooded area (if this is not common in the area), park nearby, and swimming pool. Financial features that attract interest include: owner financing, assumable 8% fixed-rate (if interest rates are above 8%), $1,000 down, rent to own.

If you are selling the house below market value you can say so in your ad. "Must sell—$8,000 discount" or "Must sell fast—$8,000 below market" or "$8,000 discount—great investment property." Readers of your ad will sense a good deal and you may have several buyers competing with each other.

For sale by owner or FSBO means they will be dealing directly with the owner. Many people like that because they feel they will get a lower price dealing directly with the owner. Since the seller doesn't have to pay a Realtor's commission, he may be willing to pass on some of the savings to the buyer. Some home buyers know they can work with an owner on things such a financing that would not be possible with a lending institution. Creative financing is discussed later in this chapter.

Owner financing, $1,000 total down, no money down, easy terms, no qualifying, and 8% fixed-rate interest are all terms you can use to attract buyers. Of course, if you advertise these terms you must be able to honor them, and you can with a little creative financing.

Showing the Property

When selling insurance or used cars it helps to be a smooth talker, but in real estate the ability to sweet talk a person into buying something is of little use. It's the property that sells, not the salesman. If the property is clean, in a decent neighborhood, and the terms are good, the home will sell itself. People will either like it or they won't.

When people come to see the house, give the best impression possible. Turn on all the lights to make the home bright and cheery. Open all the window shades or curtains.

If it's during the winter, make sure the heater is on and house is comfortable. In summer the house should be cool.

Disagreeable orders are a big turnoff, make sure the house is aired out and fresh smelling.

Let the buyers wander through the house by themselves. Don't take them on a guided tour and don't follow them. They don't need you explaining all the features, they will see for themselves. Stay in another room and let them show themselves around and let them feel at home.

Your attitude will help sell the property. If you are cheerful, positive, and show enthusiasm, the prospect will look at you and the property with a more positive frame of mind. You don't need to be pushy, but make sure to mention all selling points and finance options if they show the least bit of interest.

After looking at the property, ask them how they feel about it. If they like the house, ask them for a commitment. If they hesitate or say they need to think it over, that means they have some unanswered questions. Ask them questions about the house to discover what their concerns are. For example: Are the bedrooms big enough? Do you like the kitchen? How do you like the yard? You might want to be prepared to discuss the local schools, the proximity of major shopping centers, churches, and such. If their concerns are financial, you may be able to work some creative financing with them.

Once the prospect expresses interest in buying, your next step is to settle on the price and work out the details of closing. Before you enter into negotiations on price, remember that in a successful negotiation everybody wins. Both buyer and seller should go to the closing thinking the each got the best deal possible.

Your negotiations on price should not take the form of haggling. You are not dealing with a used car salesman. Know exactly what you are willing to sell the property for before the negotiation process begins. If the price has already been discounted, you shouldn't be expected to lower the price any further. Let him know this and work on financing instead. If the price hasn't been discounted, then you might consider lowering it. You should let the buyer feel he is getting a good deal and, yet, still leave enough for a worthwhile profit for yourself. Don't be too greedy. If you are too stubborn, you may wind up holding on to the property for a long time. You would be better off dropping the price of the house one or two thousand dollars and sell it quickly, than sticking to your price and keeping it on the market for several months. Let the house go and move on to other properties.

When terms are agreed to, the buyer will leave you an earnest money deposit as part of the down payment and as insurance that you won't sell to someone else or that he won't change his mind. The deposit can be any amount you and the buyer agree upon. If he gives you a deposit and then later decides not to buy the property, you are legally entitled to keep it as compensation for taking your property off the market. It would be unwise for you to take the property off the market before he has given you a deposit. Too many people change their minds. Once they give a deposit, they have psychologically committed themselves to purchasing the home. They understand that if they don't follow through with their commitment they will lose the deposit.

Closing

Once you've found a buyer and agreed to terms, the deal is finalized at closing.

The sale is not final until the documents are signed and you get paid. A disinterested third party handles the closing for the buyer, seller, and lender.

Closing can take place at the lender's office, such as a bank. One of the lender's employees will handle the closing, and as soon as everyone has signed the documents, you receive payment. Other places where a closing may take place, especially if the deal is owner financed, is at an escrow company, title company, or attorney's office.

Keep in mind, that until closing, you don't have a guaranteed sale. So don't go out and buy another property or some other expensive item thinking to fund it with the sale you just made. You need to wait until you have cash in hand. The reason is because the buyers may change their minds at the last minute. As the closing date approaches some buyers experience what is known as *buyer's remorse*, they get second thoughts and back out. Most all the deals you make will probably go to closing without a hitch, but be aware of the few that may want to back out at the last minute.

Unless the buyer has lots of money readily available, he is going to need financing of some type in order to purchase the property. He can get financing from a commercial lender, as most do, or you can offer to finance all or part of the transaction for him. This is were creative financing comes into play and where you have a *big* advantage over other sellers. If you are willing to help finance the sale of your property you will attract and sell many more homes, even in a buyers' market. The next section on creative financing offers several options to help you bridge the gap between showing the property and closing the deal.

CREATIVE FINANCING

In a sellers' market it is relatively easy to sell property at or near full market value and for the buyer to finance the sale with a bank or finance company. In a buyers' market you may need to rely on motivational strategies to make your property more enticing than anyone else's. With creative financing you can make your property available to many, many more people who otherwise may not be able to qualify for a conventional loan, thus drastically improving the turnover rate of your properties.

There are numerous ways you can sell property in nontraditional ways. There have been many books written on the subject. It would be to your advantage to check some out of your local library or bookstore. I will discuss a few in the following sections to give you an idea of the types of things you can do, and what others are doing.

Creative financing involves a loan where the seller participates in the lending process. There are assumptions, wraparounds, second mortgages, and many others. Creative financing is the financing of choice in a buyers' market.

Assumable Mortgages

Before I get to far into addressing creative financing I need to touch on the topic of assumable mortgages. If the mortgage is assumable (all FHA and

VA insured loans are assumable). Under a straight assumption, the buyer pays the difference between the balance on the mortgage and the sales price. If the property has a loan balance of $75,000 and the selling price is $100,000 the equity would be $25,000. The equity is the amount the seller receives from the buyer. The $70,000 loan obligation is transferred to the buyer. There is little involvement from the lending institution. You simply sign over the deed and loan to the new buyer, he pays you and you're done. This type of transfer is good because it saves the expense of closing costs for both of you. If the interest rate on the original loan is lower than the prevailing rate, this is a very strong selling point. This is a great way to buy property and allows you to easily pick up distressed property before it goes into foreclosure.

It is also a good way to sell property, however, all assumable loans carry a certain about of risk to the seller. The buyer has no risk, but when you sell on assumption, you need to be aware of some things. If the buyer defaults on the loan, the lender can also look to the seller, you, whose name is on the original loan documents, to get compensation. If you bought the property on assumption from someone else before reselling it, then the original owner may be responsible if the loan goes into default. Fortunately, few lenders go to the trouble of tracking down the former owner.

Although all government insured loans are assumable not all conventional loans are. In the early 1970s lenders started using the due-on-sale clause in their conventional mortgages to protect themselves from being locked into low interest rates for the full 30-year life of the loan. If the property ever sold again the buyer was required to refinance the loan at the current rate. This was a good deal for lenders because few homes ever remain with the original buyer for the full 30-year term of the loan. So lenders saw they could make a lot more money if the loan balance was due in full whenever it changed hands. Nowadays, most conventional mortgages have the due-on-sale clause. One way some investors have worked around the due-on-sale clause is the contract for deed.

Contract for Deed

With a contract for deed or sale on contract, you finance the sale of your house with the buyer. This way you have full control over the terms such as interest rate and amount of down payment. This is to your advantage because you can offer very attractive terms to the buyer, so much so that it would be hard for him to turn down.

You may offer the buyer an interest rate lower than the prevailing rate, or low or even no down payment. Or the buyer may not have to make his first payment for three months or anything you like.

You sell the property to the buyer without giving title at the time of sale and without notifying your lender of the transfer of the property. Your name is still on the original mortgage and you must continue to make payments, but the monthly payments you receive from the buyer should be enough to pay your mortgage and receive a worthwhile profit each month.

The advantage of this type of arrangement is that you can use any type of terms that suite both you and the buyer. The buyer does not have to qualify for a loan and he can take possession of the property immediately. No closing costs are involved.

There are, as you might expect, some disadvantage to this type of arrangement. The major disadvantage is that the new buyer is not the owner of record until all the terms of the contract are fulfilled. If you have any judgment filed against you, or go through a bankruptcy or divorce settlement and cannot make payments on your loan, there could be a lien placed on the property that would have to be paid before the seller can give clear title to the buyer even though he has fulfilled his part of the contract.

With this type of problem possible, there should be an agreed upon course of action should this situation arise. The safe course for the buyer is that he obtain title to the property as soon as he has enough equity, through appreciation and mortgage principal reduction (usually sometime between the second and fifth years), and that the seller than take back a mortgage or deed of trust to guarantee his remaining loan. But the buyer must understand that if the first lienholder calls the loan due, the buyer must at that point refinance.

In most states, if the contract for deed is recorded, it will protect the buyer sufficiently in case the seller does encounter economic setbacks down the road. If your loan is with an out-of-town lender, then the contract can be safely recorded. The lender would probably never find out that you sold the home. The due-on-sale clause in your mortgage would probably never be triggered. A great many mortgages are sold to other companies located out of state.

The buyer can also be protected if you give him a second lien on the property. The second lien would cover the contract for deed. Because the contract for deed would not be recorded in this case, the lender would not be aware of ownership transfer.

Although many investors have used these techniques, I prefer to avoid loans that are non-assumable. If you get a conventional loan, negotiate to have the due-on-sale clause deleted.

Wraparounds

A wraparound mortgage is a method of financing in which a new mortgage is placed in a subordinate or secondary position to an existing mortgage. The new mortgage, in essence, is wrapped around the original mortgage.

Wraparound mortgages can only be used if the original loan is assumable.

The new mortgage is financed by you, the seller. You keep your original mortgage and continue to make payments on it. The buyer will pay you on the mortgage you've given him and you in turn pay your mortgage to the original lender.

The obvious disadvantage of this type of situation is that you must continue to make mortgage payments to your lender even after the property is sold. You must also keep up on your payments or your lender can foreclose on the property even though the new owner has made all of his payments.

The advantage of a wraparound mortgage is that you can adjust any of the terms of sale to entice buyers. So, if someone can't qualify for a loan from a conventional lender, he can still buy the home from you. It also takes less time for the buyer to get into the home so the whole process can be over and done with rather quickly.

With this type of situation you can charge full market value for the property making even a low equity home profitable for you. Whatever terms you choose, you will arrange to have the payments made to you so you can cover your first mortgage and have enough left over for a healthy profit.

Let's assume you have a mortgage balance of $70,000 at 8% interest, and it's a FHA assumable loan. Your payments for principal and interest are $514. Taxes and insurance adds another $100, for a total payment of $614. You list the sales price at $90,000.

Let's say you are willing to use a wraparound mortgage to finance a potential buyer. If the selling price is $90,000 and you ask for $2,000 down, you will finance $88,000. Payments to you will be $646 plus $100 taxes and insurance for a total of $746. You can run an ad in the classified section of the newspaper that says something like this:

> No qualifying, owner financing, 8%, $2,000
> down. Only $746/month. 3bd, 2ba, 2car. Pleas-
> ant Valley area. 555-1234.

This ad will entice many interested buyers to give you a call.

After the sale of the property, you continue to pay $614 per month on the first mortgage. At the same time, the new buyer pays you $746 per month. The difference between what you pay and what you receive leaves you with $132 profit each month. In one year you will have gained $1,584. Over the life of a 30-year loan you would receive a total of $47,520, much more than the original $18,000 equity (less down payment) you started with.

A wraparound mortgage is a good way to recoup your initial investment (through the down payment which the buyer gives you) and earn a monthly "pension" for the life of the loan.

Second Mortgages

Say a buyer wants to buy on terms of no qualifying and wants to assume your loan. When the buyer does not have enough money to pay you for the entire amount of the equity and you don't want to use a wraparound mortgage, you can use a second non-wraparound mortgage. For example, let's say you're asking price is $90,000 for an assumable loan with interest rate of 8% with a balance of $70,000 so you have $20,000 in equity. The buyer must come up with $20,000 to assume the loan. Not many people have that kind of cash on hand. Even if he doesn't have $20,000 he can still buy the house and you can still get your full equity out of it. You can do this by having the buyer take out a second mortgage. Assumption avoids expense of closing costs for both of you, making it cheaper for a buyer to acquire your property and leaving more of a profit for you. This is an attractive situation for potential buyers.

What you can do is have the buyer put down a certain amount, say 5% of the asking price, which is $4,500, and have him get a second mortgage (second lien) from a commercial lender for $16,500 to pay you the balance of the equity. Usually, the second mortgage will be at an interest rate two to four percentage points higher than the going rate for new first mortgage loans. The second mortgage will usually be for a shorter term than the first, 10 to 20 years.

In our example, if the interest rate on the second mortgage is 12%, the combined interest rate on the entire amount of both mortgages is still only 8.8%. You find the average by multiplying the first lien amount by its interest rate, multiplying the second lien amount by its interest rate, adding the two totals, and divide the resulting amount by the total of the first and second lien amounts. See the example below:

$$\$70,000 \times 8\% = \$5,600 \text{ First lien}$$
$$\$20,000 \times 12\% = \$2,400 \text{ Second lien}$$
$$\$5,600 + \$2,400 = \$8,000 \text{ Total}$$
$$\$8,000 / \$90,000 = 8.8\%$$

If the rate you get by blending the two together is similar to the going rate for new loans, considering other costs it would take for a new loan, then this is a good way for the buyer to finance the property and for you to make the sale.

Many people don't have enough for a down payment of 10% or more. They would gladly pay a higher interest rate to have the down payment lowered. You might consider a similar deal.

Combining ideas of second mortgage described here and the wraparound mortgage you can develop a financing arrangement that is extremely attractive to potential buyers and can make you lots of money. This is called seller financed second mortgage and is described in the following section.

Seller Financed Second Mortgage

This is a very exciting option you should seriously consider. It provides unique advantages to both you and the buyer and has the potential to provide you with a monthly paycheck for the rest of your life.

In this case, you can have a similar situation as the one just described but instead of having the buyer go to a commercial lender, you can finance the second mortgage yourself. This provides a way for you to quickly recoup your expenses in obtaining the property as well as providing you with a steady monthly income.

Assume the same situation as described previously, $70,000 assumable first mortgage with $20,000 equity. You take a 5% down payment of $4,500.

Since you are financing the second mortgage, you have a great deal of leeway in your terms of sale and the financing arrangements. You can offer a low down payment or low interest loan or whatever. You can also be creative on the type of loan you offer. It doesn't have to be a fixed-rate loan, but can be a variable rate that increases each year up to a certain point (this can make it easier for someone to get into the home), balloon payment, etc.

Have an attorney draw up the loan documents for you to make sure everything is legal and you're protected from unforeseeable circumstances. Once you have the documents, you can copy them and use them in the sale of other properties.

One of the great things about this type of arrangement is that you get your initial investment back and a regular income for the life of the second mortgage, which may be 10 or 15 years or more. If you earn $100 a month, with just ten properties sold you'll get $1,000 a month in income without any additional effort on your part. You can finance your own retirement. If you continually buy and sell properties, after a few years you could very easily build up enough to be earning over a half million dollars yearly. Many people have and are doing this right now. In the coming years as more and more properties fall into distress and foreclosures climb, you will have an abundance of real estate to choose from. The opportunities have never been better.

Working your property sales this way can be the best financial option available to you. Take the same situation as described above, but instead of financing a second mortgage the buyer refinances the entire amount possible from the bank and gave you a lump sum payment of $20,000. If you invested that money in the bank you would only receive 6 or 7 maybe even as high as 9% interest. But a second mortgage is always at least 2-4 percentage points higher than the going rate. So your loan may be around 12% or more. By lending this money to the buyer at typical interest rates you are earning more than you would by putting it into other investments. And this is a safe investment. You can always get the property back if the buyer defaults on the loan. Because property values over the long run always increase, you can resell it without experiencing a loss.

You can, if necessary, even take a third mortgage if the property already has a second. A disadvantage with taking a second mortgage (or a third) is that if the buyer defaults on the first mortgage, the first lienholder will foreclose and you won't get anything.

If this situation does happen, however, there are things you can do to prevent foreclosure. If the buyer is having trouble making payments to the first mortgage holder he is probably having trouble paying you as well. In fact, he would probably stop paying you before he stops paying the bank because he probably assumes you will give him more leeway with a missed or late payment or two. Missing a payment to a big corporation with a well developed legal and financial backing and little sympathy for homeowners is a bit scary. If this situation arises, you will be the first to know. Contact the property owner immediately and find out the problem. It may be a temporary setback and all he needs is a little time to get back on his feet. Make sure he has not defaulted on the first mortgage, if he has you need to take quick action.

If it looks like the homeowner is headed for foreclosure, you have a lot of power to negotiate with him. You have the power to foreclose on him yourself. But you don't need to go that far. What you can do is handle this like any other property that is in distress. Explain all of the negative consequences that will result from foreclose—loss of property, ruined credit, deficiency judgment, embarrassment, etc. The deficiency judgment can be scary because if you do not foreclose first, you may not get a dime and you can file for a deficiency judgment against the owner yourself. So, to protect him from all these consequences you can offer to take back ownership and responsibility of the first mortgage by paying off any missed payment (included your own which he may have missed) and penalties. This should be enough compensation for him unless the property has gained in value appreciably since you sold it to him. Even then, he has almost no bargaining power because you have the power to foreclose on him. You don't want to do this because it's time consuming and you won't get much from it, but he doesn't know that. He should be happy to get out from under a legal obligation without causing himself any further harm.

In some instances after you have sold a home the homeowner will resell the property. When he does, the buyer will probably go through a conventional lender for financing and you will be paid in a lump sum the balance due on the second mortgage. You won't lose anything, but you will lose out on receiving regular monthly payments.

An Offer Nobody Can Refuse

Be creative in the terms you offer. Even in a buyers' market you can be selling property like hotcakes if you make enticing offers. Selling tactics you can use are no qualifying, assumable loan, below market price, lower interest rate, low down payment, or deferring the first few payments for awhile. Just because you sweeten the terms doesn't mean you lose out. Make adjustments. If you lower the price, raise the interest rate, or if you lower the down payment, increase the price. Do what's necessary to make the sale, but still make a reasonable profit. When the economy is slow and buyers have the advantage, property can still sell for a handsome profit using the ideas presented above.

During the recession of the mid 1980s the economy of Texas was in its worst shape in 40 years. The oil industry was hit hard and unemployment was at an all time high. Foreclosures, too, were coming in at record breaking numbers. Many homes were for sale. It was a buyers' market. Those homeowners who insisted on full market value for their homes couldn't find buyers. But those homeowners and real estate brokers who offered incentives to buyers, either as a discount on the price or some other means, were selling homes as quickly as they placed them on the market.

During this time, interest rates had fallen but were still in the double digits. An owner of a townhouse had his property up for sale for several months with no takers. He decided to change brokers and see what a new agent could do. The new broker was much more creative than the original and didn't just list the property, but went out to sell it. The owner wanted $58,900 for the property. The new real estate agent *raised* the price to $63,900 and advertised that the buyer could assume the seller's 8% FHA loan. The seller would carry a 0% interest second lien payable over 10 years with $10,000 down. The property sold in a couple of weeks.

The seller got just as much out of the property as he originally would have if he sold it under standard terms. Even though he offered 0% interest, the increase in price made up for the loss in interest.

Using similar creative financing techniques this real estate agent sold over 40 homes in three months in a depressed Texas market.

With some thought and ingenuity, you can sell your property quickly regardless of the economy. If you offer, no qualifying, low down payment or even no money down, and comfortable payments even in a tough market you will find a buyer.

Check Out the Buyer

You need to be careful when you finance a property or even when you rent. You are offering terms that aren't normally available through institutional lenders. You may emphasize easy terms and no qualifying. This type of advertising may attract people who are prone to have financial difficulty. You need to weed them out.

You want a buyer who is reliable and can make payments on time. Just like any other business that takes credit, you need to check the credit worthiness of any potential buyer. Your buyer, however, doesn't need to be able to quality for a loan from a bank to be a good credit risk. There are many reliable people who have a steady income and can afford to buy a home. You can make it possible for them to achieve this goal when they can't get bank financing.

Have the buyer fill out a credit application and read it carefully. Make sure he fills out all the banks. You need to call and check all his credit references.

The following page provides an example of a credit application you can use.

RENTAL PROPERTIES

Investing in the Future

If by chance you can't resell your property quickly, or you want to hold on to it and wait for property values to go up, you need to turn it into an income producing property by renting it out. You must rent it for enough to cover your mortgage payment and maintenance expenses. Depending on the housing market, you may even charge enough to earn a profit as well.

The idea behind renting property is that it will appreciate in value. You can then sell it later after values have increased. It takes longer to recoup your investment this way, but it is an option that is open to you.

All property increases in value. There are ups and downs in the market, but the overall trend is upwards. Real estate is the safest investment you can ever make. More and more people want land. Its a limited resource and supply and demand determines market value. While the value of property may stall for a few years it will shoot up eventually. Usually, property increases in value even in recessions, although at a slower rate. Property values may actually drop temporarily at times when the economy is very poor, but it will shoot back up past former high levels. Dramatic rises in property values can occur within a couple of years.

In some cases, homeowners may be wise to keep their property and turn them into rental properties. This is especially true in areas where properties have appreciated little in recent years, where homes are difficult to sell, and for tax shelters.

There are tax advantages to consider. Up to certain limits you can take as much as $25,000 a year in passive losses as a deduction against other income.

CREDIT APPLICATION

Borrower _____ date of birth _____ Social Security number _____
Address_____
Home phone_____ Work phone_____
Name and address of landlord or agent _____
Present rent _____ Years at present address_____
Previous address _____
Previous rent _____ Years at previous address _____
Employer (name and address)_____
Length of Employment _____ Monthly income _____ Position held _____
Other income source _____ Monthly income _____
Previous employer (name and address) _____
Length of Employment _____
Material status _____ Number of dependents _____
Co-Borrower _____ date of birth _____ Social Security number _____
Address _____
Home Phone _____ Work phone _____
Name and address of landlord or agent _____
Present rent _____ Years at present address _____
Previous address _____
Previous rent _____ Years at previous address _____
Employer (name and address)_____
Length of Employment _____ Monthly income _____ Position held _____
Other income source _____ Monthly income _____
Previous employer (name and address) _____
Length of Employment _____
Material status _____ Number of dependents _____
Bank:
Name, Address, and Phone) _____
Checking account # _____ Savings account # _____ Cash in Bank _____
Automobiles:
Make, Year, Model _____
Lender _____ Monthly payment _____
Make, Year, Model _____
Lender _____ Monthly payment _____
Make, Year, Model) _____
Lender _____ Monthly payment _____
Credit cards/ Personal Loans and other debts:
Name of creditor_____ Original debt _____
Unpaid balance _____ Monthly payment _____ Amount past due (if any) _____
Name of creditor_____ Original debt _____
Unpaid balance _____ Monthly payment _____ Amount past due (if any) _____
Name of creditor_____ Original debt _____
Unpaid balance _____ Monthly payment _____ Amount past due (if any) _____
Name of creditor_____ Original debt _____
Unpaid balance _____ Monthly payment _____ Amount past due (if any) _____
Name of creditor_____ Original debt _____
Unpaid balance _____ Monthly payment _____ Amount past due (if any) _____
Alimony or Child support obligation _____
Have you had a foreclosure or declared bankruptcy within the past 7 years?_____
Judgments _____

I authorize _____ to obtain my/our credit report for the purpose of determining credit
worthiness. The information that is obtained is strictly confidential.
I hereby certify that all statements are true and complete to the best of my knowledge and are made for the purposes for obtaining credit. I
authorize you to obtain such information as you may require concerning the statements made in this application and agree that the
application shall remain your property whether the loan is granted or not.
Borrower's signature _____ Date _____

Co-borrower's signature_____ Date _____

Sample credit application.

Passive "losses" on rental houses include annual depreciation of the house, a paper calculation you make even when the house really is increasing in value.

Depreciation on a $100,000 house would be about $3,000 a year. That deduction could be used to shelter salary or other income from taxes.

In addition, the interest paid on the old mortgage would still be deductible, as would insurance costs and any expenses incurred in repairing or fixing up the property.

Rent to Own

Many people don't even bother to look to purchase property because although they may have a steady job, they can't qualify for a loan large enough to buy a house to suit their needs and or desires. Advertise your property for rent and you may rent it, but some will jump at the chance to buy it if you offer owner financing or other enticing incentives. This is a technique you can use if the property does not sell quickly. Advertise it for rent or for sale. Anyone who shows an interest will be a potential buyer because you can make it affordable to almost anyone. What family who has been renting, perhaps living in an apartment, could pass up a seemingly once in a lifetime opportunity to buy a home without all the hassle and expense normally involved?

Even if the person decides to rent rather than buy, you can still approach him a year later with an offer to buy. You have a psychological advantage here. By this time the family has become comfortable in their new surroundings. They know the neighbors. Children are enrolled in local schools. They are comfortable where they are. They have become accustomed to the house and it now feels like "their" home. If you give them an opportunity to buy the property for a price that's similar to what they're paying in rent, how could they pass it up? Instead of saying good-by to their rent money, they could be building up equity in their home. This is a valuable asset that can be sold for a profit in the future or used to acquire a home equity loan for cash to finance other things they may need. If you present these advantages to them, few people will refuse to buy.

You may even start off by offering a potential renter an option to rent the property for a year and if they like it they can buy it at market value. As an incentive, you might offer to use part of the rent they paid towards the down payment. This isn't really a loss to you because during the year the property will probably appreciated in value and you can get a higher price. You can negotiate any number of options that would work out for the both of you to come out with a win-win situation.

RESIDENTIAL EARNEST MONEY CONTRACT

1. PARTIES: _____ (Seller)
agrees to sell and convey to_____ (Buyer)
and Buyer agrees to buy from Seller the following property situated on_____ (County),_____ (State), known
as _____ (Address).

2. PROPERTY: Lot_____, Block_____, _____ Addition, City of _____, or as described on attached exhibit, together with the following fixtures, if any: curtain rods, drapery rods, venetian blinds, window shades, screens and shutters, awnings, wall-to-wall carpeting, mirrors fixed in place, attic fans, permanently installed heating and air conditioning units and equipment, lighting and plumbing fixtures, TV antennas, mail boxes, water softeners, shrubbery and all other property owned by Seller and attached to the above described real property. All property sold by this contract is called "Property".

3. CONTRACT SALES PRICE:
A. Cash payment payable at closing..$_____
B. Note described in 4B below (the Note)...$_____
C. Sales Price payable to Seller (Sum of A and B)..$_____

4. FINANCING CONDITIONS
☐ A. This is an all cash sale; no financing in involved.
☐ B. The Note in the principal sum shown in 3B above, dated as of the Closing Date, to be executed by Buyer and payable to the order of Seller, bearing interest at the rate of _____ percent per annum from date thereof until maturity, matured unpaid principal and interest to bear interest at the rate of 10% per annum, principal and interest to be due and payable
    ☐ (1) In_____ installments of $_____ or more each, beginning on or before_____ after date of the Note, and (Check "a" or "b")
        ☐ a. continuing regularly and at the same intervals thereafter until fully paid.
        ☐ b. continuing regularly and at the same intervals thereafter until _____, 20_____, when the entire balance of principal and accrued interest shall be due and payable.
    ☐ (2) In a lump sum on or before _____ after date of the Note.
☐ C. This contract is subject to Buyer furnishing Seller evidence that Buyer has a history of good credit.

5. EARNEST MONEY: $_____ as herewith tendered and is to be deposited as Earnest Money with _____, as Escrow Agent, upon execution of the contract by both parties. Additional Earnest Money, if any, shall be deposited with the Escrow Agent on or before _____, 20_____, in the amount of $_____.

6. TITLE: Seller at Seller's expense shall furnish either:
☐ A. Owner's Policy of Title Insurance (the Title Policy) issued by _____ in the amount of the Sales Price and dated at or after closing: OR
☐ B. Complete Abstract of Title (the Abstract) certified by _____ to current date.
NOTICE TO BUYER: AS REQUIRED BY LAW, Broker advises that YOU should have the Abstract covering the Property examined by an attorney of YOUR selection, or YOU should be furnished with or obtain a Title Policy.

7. PROPERTY CONDITIONS (Check "A" or "B"):
☐ A. Buyer accepts the Property in its present condition, subject only to _____
☐ B. Buyer requires inspections and repairs required by the Property Condition Addendum (the Addendum).
Seller shall commence and complete prior to closing all required repairs at Seller's Expense.
All inspections, reports and repairs required of Seller by this contract and the Addendum shall not exceed $_____. If Seller fails to complete such requirements, Buyer may do so and Seller shall be liable up to the amount specified and the same paid from the proceeds of the sale. If such expenditures exceed the stated amount and Seller refuses to pay such excess, Buyer may pay the additional cost or accept the Property with the limited repairs and this sale shall be closed as scheduled, or Buyer may terminate this contract and the Earnest Money shall be refunded to Buyer. Broker and sales associates have no responsibility or liability for repair or replacement of any of the Property.

8. BROKER'S FEE: _____ Listing Broker (_____%) and _____ Co-Broker (_____%) as Real Estate Broker (the Broker), has negotiated this sale and Seller agrees to pay Broker in _____ (County), _____ (State), on consummation of this sale or on Seller's default (unless otherwise provided herein) a total cash fee of _____ of the total Sales Price, which Escrow Agent may pay from the sale proceeds.

9. CLOSING: The closing of the sale (the Closing Date) shall be on or before _____, 20_____, or within 7 days after objections to title have been cured, whichever date is later.

10. POSSESSION: The possession of the Property shall be delivered to Buyer on _____ in its present or required improved condition, ordinary wear and tear excepted. Any possession by Buyer prior to or by Seller after Closing Date shall establish a landlord-tenant at sufferance relationship between the parties.

11. SPECIAL PROVISIONS:
(Insert terms and conditions of a factual nature applicable to this sale, e.g. personal property included in sale[curtains, draperies, valances, etc.], prior purchase or sale of other property, lessee's surrender of possession, and the like.)

Sample cash or owner-financed contract. You can use a contract such as this one when you have a cash buyer or when you are financing the loan without a third party.

12. SALES EXPENSES TO BE PAID IN CASH AT OR PRIOR TO CLOSING:

A. Seller's Expenses:

    (1) Any inspections, reports and repairs required of Seller herein, and in the Addendum.

    (2) All cost of releasing existing loans and recording the releases, tax statements, 1/2 of any escrow fee, preparation of Deed, copies of restrictions and easements, other expenses stipulated to be paid by Seller under other provisions of this contract.

B. Buyer's Expenses: All expenses incident to any loan (e.g. preparation of Note, Deed of Trust and other loan documents, recording fees, Mortgagee's Title Policy, credit reports), 1/2 of any escrow fee, one year premium for hazard insurance unless insurance is prorated, and expenses stipulated to be paid by Buyer under other provisions of this contract.

C. If any sales expenses exceed the maximum amount herein stipulated to be paid by either party, either party may terminate this contract unless the other party agrees to pay such excess.

13. PRORATIONS: Insurance (at Buyer's option), taxes and any rents and maintenance fees, shall be prorated to the Closing Date.

14. TITLE APPROVAL: If Abstract is furnished, Seller shall deliver same to Buyer within 20 days from the effective date hereof. Buyer shall have 20 days from date of receipt of Abstract to deliver a copy of the title opinion to Seller, stating any objections to title, and only objections so stated shall be considered. If Title Policy is furnished, the Title Policy shall guarantee Buyer's title to be good and indefeasible subject only to (i) restrictive covenants affecting the Property (ii) any discrepancies, conflicts or shortages in area or boundary lines or any encroachments, or any overlapping of improvements (iii) all taxes for the current and subsequent years (iv) any existing building and zoning ordinances (v) rights of parties in possession (vi) any liens created as security for the sale consideration and (vii) any reservations or exceptions contained in the Deed in either instance, if title objections are disclosed, Seller shall have 30 days to cure the same. Exceptions permitted in the Deed and zoning ordinances shall not be valid objections to title. Seller shall furnish at Seller's expense tax statements showing no delinquent taxes and a General Warranty Deed conveying title subject only to liens securing debt created as part of the consideration, taxes for the current year, usual restrictive covenants and utility easements common to the platted subdivision of which the Property is a part and any other reservations or exceptions acceptable to Buyer. The Note shall be secured by Vendor's and Deed of Trust liens. In case of dispute as to the form of Deed, Deed of Trust or Note, such shall be upon a form prepared by the State Bar of _____ (State).

15. CASUALTY LOSS: If any part of Property is damaged or destroyed by fire or other casualty loss, Seller shall restore the same to its previous condition as soon as reasonably possible, but in any event by Closing Date, and if Seller is unable to do so without fault, this contract shall terminate and Earnest Money shall be refunded with no Broker's fee due.

16. DEFAULT: If Buyer fails to comply herewith, Seller may either enforce specific performance or terminate this contract and receive the Earnest Money as liquidated damages, one-half of which (but not exceeding the herein recited Broker's fee) shall be paid by Seller to Broker in full payment for Broker's services. If Seller is unable without fault to deliver Abstract or Title Policy or to make any non-casualty repairs required herein within the time herein specified, Buyer may either terminate this contract and receive the Earnest Money as the sole remedy, and no Broker's fee shall be earned, or extend the time up to 30 days. If Seller fails to comply herewith for any other reason, Buyer may (i) terminate this contract and receive the Earnest Money, thereby releasing Seller form this contract (ii) enforce specific performance hereof or (iii) seek such other relief as may be provided by law. If completion of sale is prevented by Buyer's default, and Seller elects to enforce specific performance, the Broker's fee is payable only if and when Seller collects damages for such default by suit, compromise, settlement or otherwise, and after first deducting the expenses of collection, and then only in an amount equal to one-half of that portion collected, but not exceeding the amount of Broker's fee.

17. ATTORNEY'S FEES: Any signatory to this contract who is the prevailing party in any legal proceeding against any other signatory brought under or with relation to this contract or transaction shall be additionally entitled to recover court costs and reasonable attorney fees from the non-prevailing party.

18. ESCROW: Earnest Money is deposited with Escrow Agent with the understanding that Escrow Agent (I) does not assume or have any liability for performance or nonperformance of any party (ii) has the right to require the receipt, release and authorization in writing of all parties before paying the deposit to any party and (iii) is not liable for interest or other charge on the funds held. If any party unreasonably fails to agree in writing to an appropriate release of Earnest Money, then such party shall be liable to the other parties to the extent provided in paragraph 17. At closing, Earnest Money shall be applied to any cash down payment required, next to Buyer's closing costs and any excess refunded to Buyer. Before Buyer shall be entitled to refund of Earnest Money, any actual expenses incurred or paid on Buyer's behalf shall be deducted therefrom and paid to the creditors entitled thereto.

19. REPRESENTATIONS: Seller represents that there will be no Title I liens, unrecorded liens or Uniform Commercial Code liens against any of the Property on Closing Date. If any representation above is untrue this contract may be terminated by Buyer and the Earnest Money shall be refunded without delay. Representations shall survive closing.

20. AGREEMENT OF PARTIES: This contract contains the entire agreement of the parties and cannot be changed except by their written consent.

21. CONSULT YOUR ATTORNEY: This is intended to be a legally binding contract. READ IT CAREFULLY. If you do not understand the effect of any part, consult your attorney BEFORE signing. The Broker cannot give you legal advice only factual and business details concerning land and improvements. Attorneys to represent parties may be designated below, and, so employment may be accepted, Broker shall promptly deliver a copy of this contract to such attorneys.

Seller's Atty:_____ Buyer's Atty:_____

EXECUTED in multiple originals effective the _____ day of _____, 20_____

Buyer _____ Seller _____

Receipt of $_____ Earnest Money is acknowledged in the form of _____

Escrow Agent _____ By_____Date _____

9

SETTING UP BUSINESS

The purpose of this chapter is to provide you with the steps necessary to set up and establish your real estate business. You can buy and sell real estate without having to go through the motions of formally establishing a business, but if you do, you will miss out on some important tax advantages. And you will miss out on some business opportunities because people are more inclined to do business with you if you are associated with a company, even if you are the only employee. So, it is in your best interest to operate under a business enity. This is not hard nor does it take much extra effort, but it well worth it.

If you've been self-employed or are familiar with the operation and management of a business you might want to skip this chapter or just scan through it. My objective here is not to make you an accountant, but simply help you set up a functional and legal business enity.

TYPE OF BUSINESS

One of the first decisions you must make when you start a business is to determine which of the three basic types of business entities to use—sole proprietorship, partnership, or corporation. There are legal and tax considerations that enter into this decision.

A sole proprietorship is the simplest form of business organization and the easiest to operate, especially if you work out of your home. With a sole proprietorship, you *are* the business. You have total control and responsibility of how the company is financed and how it functions. All profits the company makes are yours, but so are the losses. You are also personally responsible for all of the company's debts and liabilities, which means that if your company cannot pay an obligation, the creditor can go after your personal assets to satisfy this debt. When you figure your taxable income for the year, you must add any profit, or subtract any loss, you have from your business. This is reported on a form Schedule C, *Profit or Loss From Business*, and included with your tax return Form 1040. Most businesses are sole proprietorships.

A partnership is a relationship between two or more persons who join together to carry on a trade or business. Each person contributes money, property, labor, or skill, and expects to share in the profits and losses of the business. Many small businesses can increase their assets, have access to useful equipment, and pool the skills and talents of two or more individuals in a partnership that can make the business more successful. Partnerships must file their taxes on Form 1065, *U.S. Partnership Return of Income*. This requires more time and energy to prepare than the form for the sole proprietor. A joint undertaking to share expenses or the mere co-ownership of property that is used in the business is not a partnership. A spouse or children, for example, who help out in the business are not necessarily partners even though they may be compensated for their labors. A partnership can be formed with a verbal agreement, however, it is best to have a formal signed contract. This document specifies what has been invested by each partner and exactly what is expected from them and by them.

Corporations are normally owned by a group of people who are called shareholders. The shareholders run the company through a board of directors. Officers and employees of the corporation may also be shareholders or members of the board of directors. Corporations are entitled to special tax deductions not available to sole proprietors or partnerships, but because they are considered separate entities from their owners, the corporate profits are taxed. Because of this, owners of small corporations could end up paying more taxes than sole proprietors or partnerships. One of the primary advantages of using a corporation is that shareholders cannot be held responsible for the company's debts and liabilities. This gives owners some degree of protection not given to other types of businesses. If the business goes bankrupt, it is not reflected in the owner's credit report. Also, legal judgments against the corporation are limited to the business, and lawyers usually cannot go after individual shareholders to satisfy debts. A major disadvantage is that corporations are more closely regulated by the government, and the paperwork for starting and maintaining this type of business is an unnecessary burden to many entrapenures.

A special type of corporation designed primarily for smaller businesses is an *S corporation*. This type of corporation allows small businesses to benefit from many of the advantages of being incorporated—including protection from liability—without overburdening them with regulations and paperwork. Since this entity was designed for small businesses, the government has put a limit on the maximum number of shareholders or owners an S corporation can have. In many states it is possible for a husband and wife team to satisfy requirements and form an S corporation. However, the amount of work required and expense of setting up and maintaining the business, which includes many bothersome tax forms and additional taxes sole proprietors and partnerships don't have to deal with, makes incorporating unattractive to most one- and two-person businesses.

If you are running a business by yourself or with your spouse and family, a sole proprietorship is probably the best type of business for you. Keeping your business simple allows you to devote more of your time to making it successful and less time (and frustration) with government regulations and paperwork. However, for individuals in businesses with a high possibility of being sued or in need of raising capital, an S corporation provides some peace of mind because personal assets and credit records are protected. For more detailed information about the three basic types of business and what is required for each, I recommend that you get a copy of the IRS Publication 334, *Tax Guide for Small Business*. This book is essential for anybody starting up a new business. It describes in detail what records must be kept, what deductions are allowed, and how to fill out the various tax forms, and includes many valuable examples. Reading this book should be one of the first things you do before you start up your business. The book is free and you can pick it up at your nearest IRS office or request a copy by mail.

BUSINESS NAME

Who would you rather sell or buy your home from Frank Snorkel or Snorkel Real Estate Investment Company? The only difference is the name, but people will be far more inclined to deal with a business than they would an individual. A person who approaches you in an official capacity as part of a business enenty comes across as more legitimate and trustworthy than simply an individual seeking to buy property.

One of the first things to consider when starting a new business is choosing a name. This can be fun, but you should choose a name with care. I recommend that you pick a name that is simple and easy to pronounce. You don't want people to avoid mentioning your business because the name is difficult or uncomfortable to say. You should also select a name that describes your business, so that potential clients and business associates can easily identify what you do. You may simply use your own name or a part of your name in combination with some descriptive term, such as "William Gordon, Investor", "Gordon Investments, "Gordon and Associates." You may also choose a name unrelated to your own given name, such as "Metropolitan Real Estate Ventures" or "Los Angeles Investment Properties."

As these examples show, you can tag words onto the end of your name such as investments, associates, enterprises, and the like. But you need to be careful with some terms. The word "enterprises" is one of these. Because enterprises can be used with most any type of business, it has been over-used, particularly by one-person businesses and other very small companies. As a result, the word now has become synonymous with "amateur." If you want to avoid being automatically classified as an inexperienced one-person business, you should avoid this term. Other words you should not use are corporation (Corp.), incorporated (Inc.), and limited (Ltd.). These terms all denote a corporation, and your business should be legally incorporated before you use them.

Once you have chosen a name, you must go to your local county clerk's office (this is usually in the county courthouse), register your business name and get a Fictitious Name Statement. This is discussed in more detail later in this chapter under the heading "Licenses and Permits".

If you use your own name as a part of your company name, such as John Smith Company, in most places you are not required to get a Fictitious Name Statement. Many localities will waive the registration, even if only your last name is included in the business name. So, Nelson Investment Services would not need to be registered. Check with your local county clerk's office to see what the requirements are in your area.

BUSINESS LOCATION AND ADDRESS

Another important consideration is choosing a business location and address. The two may not be the same. If you work out of your home, your first thought may be to use your home address for business. Although there is nothing wrong with working out of the home, in some types of businesses home-based workers are not taken as seriously or considered as professional or successful as those who can afford an outside office. This is sometimes the case with real estate investors. However, many successful investors do work out of their homes. Many realtors and others in real estate industry frequently work out of their homes. Most people realize this and show no prejudice.

Unless you already rent an office outside your home for other purposes, working out of your home is the most convenient and cost effective route you can take. Renting a separate office, especially when you are first starting out and income is at its lowest, is generally an unnecessary luxury and expense.

There are many advantages of working out of a home-based office. Convenience is obviously one of the prime benefits. You can spend as much time at the office as you need with all the conveniences of home. You waste no time commuting to and from work. You have instant access to business records and materials 24 hours a day. Overhead expenses are low. You can take time to attend young children or fill other obligations throughout the day. You are also entitled to some important tax deductions. You can deduct as business expenses a part of your rent and household costs, such as trash removal, gas, and electricity.

If you work at home, you should be aware of zoning laws although it will have little affect on your real estate invesment business. Due to zoning laws, technically it is illegal in many residential areas to operate a business out of the home. The zoning laws were established to protect homeowners from businesses that create a lot of noise, attract crowds, or produce offensive odors. Some areas require home-based businesses located in residential zones to obtain some kind of "conditional use," or "special-use" permit. Many home-based workers have challenged zoning laws that prohibit or restrict home businesses and, although they have not always been successful, they have usually been allowed to continue to work at home without legal reprisals so long as there are no complaints from area residents. Barbara Brabec in her book, *Homemade Money,* explains that home-based workers have been able to avoid zoning conflicts by using a post office box as a business address. Since the post office is located in a commercial zone, the business is considered part of that zone. But again, there must not be complaints from the neighbors. The point to this is that, if you don't disturb your neighbors and no one complains about what you are doing, in most cases you can work out of your home regardless of the zoning laws. As a real estate investor, you should not be a nuisance to your neighbors and, therefore, do not need to worry about violating your local zoning laws.

If, however, you buy and sell a lot of personal property obtained from bankruptcies, estate sales, and the like, you need to be aware of zoning laws. If you bring in a lot of merchandise and have customers come to you home to look it over, this may cause problems. I knew one person who bought merchandise and sold it a garage sales. He would a new garage sale every couple of weeks. I think his neighbors got real tired of this after awhile.

You can make your home office appear more businesslike by having a separate business address—one that is not obviously a residential address (e.g., Artistic Cir., Silent Rain Rd., Chestnut Ct., Bluebird Pl., Colony Hills Ln.). This can be done by renting a postal box. Also, if you live in an apartment or move frequently, a postal box provides stability. Some people do not like to use a post office box because they feel it appears less legitimate. The belief is that con artists frequently use them rather than reveal their residence address. This may have been so at one time, but it really isn't true anymore. A great many businesses use post office boxes for their mailing addresses. Because so many businesses use postal boxes nowadays, there is little prejudice against it. In fact, a post office box can make you look more businesslike because you are not using an obvious residential address.

If you don't want to use your residential address and don't want to use a post office box number, you can use a private postal box. These are very popular because you use the street address where the postal box office is located and a suite number to designate your box number. This way it appears as if your mailing address is an office, rather than a postal box. The cost to rent a private postal box is a little more than a post office box. Private postal boxes can be found in most any moderate-sized city. Look in the phone book under "Mailing Service" for one in your area.

If you are relatively stable in your present location, your residential address looks like it could be a business address, and you do not disturb your neighbors, it is cheaper and easier just to use your residential address.

LICENSES AND PERMITS

Before you can go into business, you must conform to all government laws and regulations. Most licenses and permits are regulated by local governments: city, county, and state. You can expect to pay something for the licenses and permits you need. Fees can run anywhere from $10 to as much as $100 or more. Some home-based businesses ignore these requirements and get away with it, but it is too much of a risk and limits the amount of exposure you can get. If you get too much publicity or too much business, someone is going to find out and you could be hit with a heavy fine or put out of business.

Trade Name Registration

If your business goes by a name other than your own name, you will need to get a fictitious name, also known as DBA, which is an acronym for "doing business as." If you do business under a fictitious name, you are required to register the name in the county in which you do business. This prevents other businesses in the county from doing business under the same name.

Before your name can be registered, it must be checked with all the other business names in the county. If the name you have chosen, or a very similar name, is already registered by someone else, you will need to pick another name. If you live in a large metropolitan area, you may find that your first choice is already being used and maybe even your second and third. So you might want to have a few names selected, just in case your first choice is not available. When your business name is cleared and registered, you will receive a Fictitious Name Statement that allows you to do business under that name. In addition to registering your name, you will be required to publish a notice of your business name in a general circulation newspaper. Any advertisement you may plan to run in the paper would satisfy this requirement. But you can fulfill this requirement by placing a small, inexpensive classified ad. The county clerk may even provide you with a list of local newspapers which carry such ads. The cheapest papers to advertise in are usually local shopper guides which are devoted almost entirely to advertising.

Registration of your trade name is good for anywhere from five to 10 years, depending on your locality, after which time you will need to renew your registration. If you don't renew your registration, another person can claim your business name and you will be forced to change your company name. Most county offices do not bother to send renewal notices, so you will have to keep track of when your registration expires. Contact your county clerk's office for details.

Business License

Besides the Fictitious Name Statement, most places require businesses to get a local business license. Businesses which use a fictitious name usually must get their Fictitious Name Statement first. All types of businesses are required to get a license. Some occupations, such as accountants, lawyers, chiropractors, doctors, and other professionals are expected to have educational qualifications and are required to pass a test before a license is issued. But for most businesses, including real estate investment or general retail and wholesale sales, no special tests or certifications are required. Business licenses are renewed every year or two.

Sales Tax Permit

Every state which has a sales tax issues a sales tax permit. If all you are going to do is buy and sell real estate you need not bother with this. But if you deal in any merchandise you will need to get a sales tax permit and collect sales tax from your retail customers. For more information on the sales tax requirements in your area, contact your state and city revenue offices.

Better Business Bureau

Some people may be suspicious when you come to them asking to buy their property or when you offer to finance a home loan. Since you are an individual, they don't know if you're ligimate or some con artist. Representing a business that has a business address helps to convince them that you are a legimate investor. Another thing that helps is to be registered with the Better Business Bureau.

Before doing business with new companies, some people will check with the Better Business Bureau. If the companies are registered and have no complaints filed against them, it is assumed the businesses are legitimate and operating in a proper manner. You can increase your credibility by registering with your local bureau. To register, take your business license down to your local BBB and fill out an application. That's all there is to it. Being registered and having no complaints may be the key that will help you land that important deal. Let your prospects know you are registered with the BBB and encourge them to call.

BANK ACCOUNT

Most businesses should have a separate checking account rather than use a personal account. This is more important with a business that deals with a lot of merchandise than it is with real estate. The reason for keeping your business and personal finances separate is to have an accurate record of your business finances. Combining the two will only get you confused later on, when you're trying to figure your taxes or your company's financial situation.

If you have chosen a business name other than your own name, you will need to add this name to your bank account so you can deposit checks written out to your business, and so you can get checks with your business name printed on them. The bank needs to know that you and your business are the same, and for verification they will need to see the Fictitious Name Statement you obtained at the county courthouse.

Some banks allow self-employed customers to put their business name on their personal checking account. In this case you can have two personal accounts—one for personal use and one for business. This is the most economical option. Other banks may require you to have an actual business account. This is okay, except that banks usually charge businesses additional or higher processing fees and minimum balances are usually larger, so it will cost you a little more for a business account. Shop around for a bank that will let you use a personal account for your business or one that has the most economical terms for their business accounts.

LETTERHEADS AND ENVELOPES

An important part of your business success depends on the image you present. The way you present yourself influences what people think of you. If you try to look and act like an experienced professional, you will be perceived as one, even if you are a beginner. As a professional, more people will be interested in dealing with you.

One of the best ways to project a positive image is to have professionally-designed letterheads, matching envelopes, and business cards printed using your business name. I stress "professionally-designed" because too many self-employed individuals give little thought to designing a logo or letterhead, and their designs shout "amateur!" Have a graphic artist design your logo and letterhead or ask your printer for suggestions. He may have several suitable styles for you to choose from.

Printed stationery is important because it conveys the image that you are a successful professional. It is important to present a proper business appearance and attitude. Include your business name, mailing address, and phone number on all your stationery.

You will be writing letters to homeowners expressing your interest in buying their property, so you want to convey a professional appearence from the start.

Business cards should be handed out like candy. Give them out to everyone and tell them what you do. Include on the card a sentence or two describing your business. Just saying William Gordon, Investor, doesn't tell a person anything. Add discriptive line like, "I buy and sell real estate" or "I sell real estate—no money down, no qualifying".

TELEPHONE

The telephone is an essential part of your business. It is the means in which most of your contacts will be made. If you work in an office outside the home you might consider using that phone number. For most people who work for someone else, this isn't always practical. Your home phone may be your best option.

Most home-based businesses use their residential lines for their business. After all, why pay extra for another phone line when one is already available? I don't recommend this. Phone regulations in each state vary and in some states it is illegal to use your personal line in a business. Depending on your state regulations, you may simply be asked to stop, or you may be charged business phone rates, or be hit with a hefty fine. If you print your phone number on your stationery and business cards (as you should), in advertisements, and answer the phone with a business name, sooner or later you will be discovered. Call your local phone company to find out what the regulations are in your area.

Using your residential phone in your business does not qualify it for a tax deduction. The first phone line in the home cannot be used as a tax deduction. A second line can be fully deductible if it is used primarily for your business. In states where business can be conducted over a residential line, you can have two personal lines and designate one as your business line. Of course, all long-distance business calls are deductible regardless of which phone is used.

The phone you use in business should be answered with the business name and not with a simple "Hello." This is all part of conducting yourself in a businesslike manner and conveying a professional image. If one of your children answers the phone, the caller may think he has the wrong number or question if you are running a serious business. This may cause a prospect to go elsewhere. You cannot simply tell your family not to answer the phone during certain hours. Calls are not restricted to just business hours or on weekdays. Although most business calls come during normal working hours, you may receive calls at any hour and on weekends and holidays.

If you seriously get into buying and selling real estate or personal property or get involved in any other type of business, I recommend that you get a separate business line regardless of the state regulations. One major advantage of having a business line is that your phone number will be listed in the business section of the phone book. People looking for businesses of all types usually look in the phone book first. Plus, local and out-of-state callers can get in touch with you by asking for directory assistance. Not having a business listing is a serious mistake because it will stifle business opportunities and prevent many potential clients from getting in contact with you. Although the monthly fee for a business phone is a little higher, there is no additional charge for the basic yellow page listing. The small extra cost of having a business line is well worth it.

Have your name listed under "Real Estate." If you buy and sell merchandise select a heading which best describes the products you deal with such as "tools", "sporting goods", "toys", etc. or even under "swap shops".

Don't let the telephone sales represenative try to talk you into getting a larger ad. In most cases you won't need it and it is an unnecessary expense. The basic listing that all customers are entitled to is enough. This listing is normally limited to just two lines containing your business name, address, and phone number. You may be able to add a tag line to your business name if it can be put all on one line. For example, "Smith Properties—Buy, Sell, Trade", or "Investment Properties—Buy and Sell." If you sell personal property you may use terms like "new and used" or "surplus merchandise."

You have three options available to you: (1) add a business line (the best option), (2) use a second personal line for business (if state laws permit), or (3) remove your personal line and install a single business line. The third option avoids the cost of having a second line and gets your company listed in the *Yellow Pages*. However, as a signle line, you cannot deduct the basic phone cost on your taxes and you must constantly regulate who answers the phone.

Another consideration you need to make is using an answering machine or answering service. Having an answering machine is important to a one-person business since you cannot be home all the time to answer your phone. With an answering machine, clients can leave messages with assurance that their calls will be returned.

RECORD KEEPING AND TAXES

Bookkeeping

Bookkeeping is an often dreaded but necessary aspect of business. You must keep accurate records not only for tax purposes, but to help you operate your business. Many of your business decisions will be based on your financial records. Carefully reviewing these records may be the only way you will really know if you're making a profit or not. Many business failures have been attributed to poor record-keeping. This is particularly important with home-based businesses, where personal and business finances can become mixed and confused.

Keeping an accurate financial record is not really difficult. You do not need an accountant to keep your books. All you need to do is keep a daily record of all your business income and expenses. Buy a ledger book at an office supply store to record expenses and income. Every time you have a business expense or receive payment, write it down. Write it down that day; do not wait or you may forget to enter it. Keeping your records accurate should be a daily practice that should take you only a few minutes.

All business transactions should be made through your business checking account. When you receive a payment, deposit it in your account. Pay all your business expenses with a business check. This way your income and expenses are easily recorded and well-documented. You may not, however, be able to pay all of your expenses by check. Some payments will have to be in cash, such as a parking fee. Make sure that these expenses are recorded in your expense ledger and receipts are kept for everything, including credit card purchases.

Keep a file and put all of your receipts in it. You must have proof for each expense you claim as a deduction. If you are audited, you will be required to produce these receipts. You will need to keep these records for at least three years because audits can go back that far.

For income tax purposes, you have to choose an accounting method. The two primary accounting methods are cash and accrual. One of these methods is chosen when you file your first tax return for your business. After that, you must use the same method every year. If you want to change your accounting method, you must first get permission from the IRS.

The cash method of accounting is used by most individuals and many small, service-oriented businesses. If you sell merchandise you are required to use the accrual method.

In the cash method of accounting, income is recorded when cash is received and expenses are recorded when paid. Cash is defined as currency, checks, and money orders. All credit purchases and sales are not recorded until payment is received. This is an easy method of accounting, but not totally representative of your financial situation because you may have debts or unpaid credit accounts that are not taken into consideration.

In the accrual method of accounting, income and expenses are recorded when they are incurred, regardless of when they are paid. If you bill a customer, you will record it in your income ledger as income. When you make a credit purchase, you will record that as an expense when the purchase is made and not when it is paid.

As a real estate investment business, most of your income is received on a cash basis, so it is better for you to use the cash method of accounting. If you also sell merchandise you will need to use the accrual method.

Taxes

You can deduct, on your income tax return, any expenses related to operating your business—postage, stationery, typing or other services you use, travel expenses, gasoline usage, phone, insurance, advertising, bad debts, professional services, taxes and licenses, etc. Any business expense is legitimate. If you have an office in your home, exclusively set aside for your business, you can deduct the rent or part of the mortgage payment for that portion of your home. You also can deduct a portion of your expenses for household utilities (water, electricity, gas). To do this, though, the room must be used exclusively for your business and nothing else.

Your total business income is figured by subtracting all your business expenses from your business income. One advantage of being self-employed is that a net loss in your business can offset other income. For example, if at year end you had a net loss of $5,000 from your investment business, but earned $40,000 as an employee in another business, your total income would be $35,000. If you own rental properties you can deduct depriciation expenses. This is a paper expense rather than a real expense because the property, in reality, is appreciating in value, but you get to deduct it as an expense. This makes owning real estate an attractive investment.

To prevent people from claiming business losses every year as a result of an activity that is really a hobby rather than a legitimate business, the IRS has put some limitations on the self-employed. To use a net loss to offset other income, a business must keep accurate records, conduct itself in a businesslike manner, and make a profit in at least three out of five consecutive years.

In spite of some business owner's best efforts, a profit may not be realized in the time specified. For this reason, the IRS has allowed some exceptions to the three-years-of-profit test. The determining factors will be if your activity is carried on in a businesslike manner, you spend adequate time to make it successful, income is used for your livelihood, you have adequate experience in this activity, and you can expect to make a profit in the future.

There are also tax considerations of which you should be aware. One of the major benefits of owning real estate is the tax deductions that can be taken on the interest payments.

Prepayment penalties (which are considered interest payments) are fully tax deductable in the year they are paid. Points paid in refinancing are also deductable if you are buying or refinancing a home. If the property you are refinancing is not your residence but an investment, then money paid for points must be slowly deducted over the entire life of the loan or until the property is sold.

For further information on business deductions and how to figure your net income or loss, I highly recommend that you read the IRS publication, *Tax Guide for Small Business* (Publication 334) and *Business Use of Your Home* (Publication 587). You need to do this before you start spending any money in your business so you will be aware of what you can and what you can't deduct, and what will be expected of you when you figure your income tax return.

Because you are self-employed, you will not receive W-2 forms. W-2 forms are given by businesses to employees. Because you do not have an employeer taking part of your salary out to pay for taxes, you need to reserves some of the money you earn for this purpose. If you earn a substantial amount, your tax obligation could be significant. To ease the burden of paying a large amount of taxes at the end of the year, the IRS requires payment of estimated taxes. These are paid quarterly throughout the tax year. The IRS provides form 1040ES for this purpose.

FORECLOSURE LAW CITATIONS

ALABAMA
Code of Alabama, Vol. 5, Title 6, Sections 6-5-240 et seq.; Vol. 19 Title 35 Sections 35-10-1 et seq.

ALASKA
Alaska Statutes, Vol. 2 Title 9, Sections 09.45.170 et seq.; Title 34, Sections 34.20.070 et seq.

ARIZONA
Revised Statutes Annotated, Vol. 4A, Title 12, Sections 12-1281 et seq.; Vol. 11, Title 33, Sections 33-721 et seq.; 33-807

ARKANSAS
Arkansas Statutes Annotated, Vol. 5, Sections 51-1105 et seq.; Vol. 7B, Sections 84-1201

CALIFORNIA
California Civil Code Sections 2920 et seq.; 2945 et seq.; 1695 et seq.

COLORADO
Colorado Revised Statutes 1973, Vol. 16, Title 38, Sections 38-37-101 et seq.; 38-39-101 et seq.

CONNECTICUT
Connecticut General Statutes Annotated, Vol. 22A, Section 49-14, 49-17 et seq.

DELAWARE
Delaware Code Annotated, Vol. 6, Sections 10-4716, 10-4961 et seq.; 10-5061 et seq.

FLORIDA
Florida Statutes Annotated, Vol. 2, Section 45.031; Vol. 20, Section 702.01

GEORGIA
Georgia Code Annotated, Book 20, Sections 67-115 et seq.; 67-201, 67-401, 67-701, 67-1503 et seq.

HAWAII
Hawaii Revised Statuted, Vol. 7A, Sections 677-1 et seq.

IDAHO
Idaho Code, Vol. 2, Sections 5-226 et seq., 6-101, 11-301 et seq., 11-401

ILLINOIS
Illinois Code of Civil Procedure, Sections 12-122 et seq., 15-101 et seq.

INDIANA
Burns' Indiana Statutes Annotated, Sections 32-8-16-1, 32-8-17-1, 34-1-39-4 et seq., 34-2-29-3

IOWA
Iowa Code Annotated, Vol. 50, Sections 628.2 et seq., 654.1

KANSAS
Kansas Statutes Annotated, Vol. 4, Sections 58-2253 et seq., 58-2314, et seq.; Vol. 4A, Sections 60-2410 et seq.

KENTUCKY
Baldwin's Kentucky Revised Statutes, Vol. 7, Sections 426.200 et seq.

LOUISIANA
Louisiana Revised Statutes, Vol. 6, Article 2343, Vol. 10, Article 2568 Code of Civil Procedure; Vol. 7 4106, 4341 et seq.; Vol. 8 4942 et seq.

MAINE
Maine Revised Statutes Annotated, Vol. 7, Sections 14-2151, 14-2202 et seq., 14-2251 et seq., Vol. 8, Sections 14-6201 et seq.

MARYLAND
Annotated Code of Maryland, Vol. 9C, Rule W70 et seq, BR6

MASSACHUSSETTS
Annotated Laws of Massachuetts, Chapter 244, Section 244-1 et seq., 244-17A, 244-35

MICHIGAN
Michigan Statutes Annotated, Vol. 22, Sections 27A.3140, 27A.3201 et seq.

MINNESOTA
Milnnesota Statutes Annotated, Vol 37, Section 580.02 et seq., 581.10 582.14 et seq.

MISSISSIPPI
Mississippi Code 1972 Annotated, Vol. 5, Section 15-1-19 et seq.; Vol. 19, Section 89-1-53 et seq.

MISSOURI
Vernon's Annotated Missouri Statutes, Vol. 23, Sections 443.290 et seq.

MONTANA
Montana Code Annotated 1981, Vol. 3, Sections 25-13-801 et seq.

NEBRASKA
Revised Statutes of Nebraska, Vol. 2, Sections 25-1530, 25-2137 et seq.

NEVADA
Nevada Revised Statutes, Vol. 2, Sections 21.130 et seq.; Vol. 3, Section 40.430; Vol. 5, Sections 106.025, 107.080 et seq.

NEW HAMPSHIRE
New Hampshire Revised Statutes Annotated, Vol. 4A, Sections 479.19 et seq.; Vol. 5, Section 529.26

NEW MEXICO
New Mexico Statutes 1978 Annotated, Vol. 6, Sections 39-5-1, 39-5-19 et seq., Vol. 7, Sections 48-3-14, 48-7-7

NEW YORK
Mckinney's Consolidated Laws of New York Annotated, Book 49 1/2, Sections 1352, 1401 et seq.

NORTH CAROLINA
General Statutes of North Carolina, Vol. 1, Sections 1-47; Vol. 2A, Sections 45-21.1 et seq.

NORTH DAKOTA
North Dakota Century Code Annotated, Vol. 5A, Sections 28-24-01 et seq.; Vol. 6, Section 32-19-1, 32-19-18; Vol. 7, Sections 35-22-01 et seq.

OHIO
Page's Ohio Revised Code Annotated, Title 23, Section 2323

OKLAHOMA
Oklahoma Statutes Annotated, Section 12-686, 12-764, 46-31 et seq., 46-301

OREGON
Oregon Revised Statutes, Vol. 1, Sections 86-010, 86-710 et seq., 88-040 et seq.

PENNSYLVANIA
Purdon's Pennsylvania Statutes Annotated, Title 72, Sections 403 et seq., 59710

RHODE ISLAND
General Laws of Rhode Island, Vol. 6, Sections 34-23-1 et seq., 34-26-1, 34-27-1, et seq.

SOUTH CAROLINA
Code of Laws of South Carolina 1976, Vol. 7, Sections 15-39-640 et seq., Vol. 10, Section 29-3-10, 29-3-630 et seq.

SOUTH DAKOTA
South Dakota Codified Laws 1967, Vol. 6, Section 15-19-23; Vol. 7, Sections 21-52-2 et seq.

TENNESSEE
Tennessee Code Annotated, Vol. 4, Sections 16-16-111, 21-1-803, 35-501 et seq., 66-8-101

TEXAS
Vernon's Civil Statutes of the State of Texas Annotated, Vol. 12, Title 56, Articles 3810, 3819 et seq.; 1982 Texas Rules of Court, Rule #309

UTAH
Utah Code Annotated 1953 (1977), Vol. 9A, Sections 78-37-1, 78-40-8; Vol. 9B, Rules of Civil Procedure 69(e) 1-3, 69(f) 1-5

VERMONT
Vermont Statutes Annotated, Title 12, Sections 12-4529 et seq., Rules of Civil and Appellate Procedudre 80.1 (e) (h)

VIRGINIA
Code of Virginia, Vol. 8, Sections 55-59 et seq.

WASHINGTON
Revised Code of Washington Annotated, Title 6, Sections 6.24.010 et seq.; Title 61, Section 61.12.060

WEST VIRGINIA
West Virginia Code, Vol. 11, Sections 38-1-1A et seq.; Vol. 16, Sections 59-3-1 et seq.

WISCONSIN
West's Wisconsin Statutes Annotated, Section 815.31, 846.51 et seq.

WYOMING
Wyoming Statutes Annotated, Vol. 2, Sections 1-18-101 et seq.; Vol. 7, Sections 34-4-102 et seq.

DIRECTORY OF HUD OFFICES*

ALABAMA
Daniel Building
15 South 20th Street
Birmingham, Alabama 35233
(205) 254-1617

ALASKA
701 "C" Street, Box 64
Anchorage, Alaska 99513
(907) 271-4170

ARIZONA
1 North First Avenue, Suite 400
Phoenix, Arizona 85004
(602) 261-4156

Arizona Bank Building
100 North Stone Avenue, Suite 410
Tucson, Arizona 85701
(602) 629-5220

ARKANSAS
Lafayette Building
523 Louisiana Street, Suite 200
Little Rock, Arkansas 72201
(501) 378-5401

CALIFORNIA
Phillip Burton Federal Building
450 Golden Gate Avenue
Post Office Box 36003
San Francisco, California 94102
(415) 556-4752

1630 East Shaw Ave, Suite 200
Fresno, California 93710
(209) 487-5036

1615 West Olympic Blvd.
Los Angeles, California 90015
(213) 251-7122

777 12th Street, Suite 200
Sacramento, California 95814
(916) 551-1351

Federal Office Building
880 Front Street, Rm 5-S-3
San Diego, California 92188
(619) 557-5310

34 Civic Center Plaza
Box 12850
Santa Ana, California 92712
(714) 836-2451

COLORADO
Executive Tower Building
1405 Curtis Street
Denver, Colorado 80202
(303) 837-4513

CONNECTICUT
330 Main Street, First Fl.
Hartford, Connecticut 06106
(203) 240-4523

DELAWARE
844 King Street, Rm. 1304
Wilmington, Delaware 19801
(302) 573-6300

DISTRIC OF COLUMBIA
451 Seventh St. S.W. Rm 3158
Washington, D.C. 20410
(202) 453-4500

FLORIDA
Gables 1 Tower
1320 South Dixie Highway
Coral Gables, Florida 33146
(305) 662-4500

*Also includes FNMA and FHLMC offices.

325 West Adams Street
Jacksonville, Florida 32202
(904) 791-2626

Langley Building
3751 Maguire Blvd., Suite 270
Orlando, Florida 32803
(407) 648-6441

700 Twiggs Street, Rm 527
Post Office Box 172910
Tampa, Florida 33672
(813) 228-2501

GEORGIA
Richard B. Russell Federal Building
75 Spring Street, SW
Atlanta, Georgia 30303
(404) 221-5136

HAWAII
300 Ala Moana Blvd.
Post Office Box 50007
Honolulu, Hawaii 96813
(808) 546-1343

IDAHO
Federal Building
Post Office Box 042
550 West Fort Street
Boise, Idaho 83724
(208) 334-1990

ILLINOIS
300 South Wacker Drive
Chicago, Illinois 60606
(312) 353-5680

547 West Jackson Blvd.
Chicago, Illinois 60606
(312) 353-7660

524 South Second Street, Rm 600
Springfield, Illinois 62701
(217) 492-4085

INDIANA
151 North Delaware Street
Indianapolis, Indiana 46204
(317) 269-6303

IOWA
Federal Building
210 Walnut Street, Room 259
Des Moines, Iowa 50309
(515) 284-4512

KANSAS
444 SE Quincy Street, Room 297
Topeka, Kansas 66683
(913) 295-2683

KENTUCKY
539 Fourth Avenue
Post Office Box 1044
Louisville, Kentucky 40201
(502) 582-5251

LOUISIANA
1661 Canal Street
New Orleans, Louisiana 70112
(504) 569-7200

New Federal Building
500 Fannin Street
Shreveport, Lousisiana 71101
(318) 226-5385

MAINE
23 Main St., First Floor
Bangor, Maine 04401
(207) 945-0467

MARYLAND
The Equitable Building
10 North Calvert Street
Baltimore, Maryland 21202
(301) 962-2520

MASSACHUSETTS
Thomas P. O'Neil, Jr.
Federal Building
10 Causeway St., Rm 375
Boston, Massachusetts 02222
(617) 565-5234

Bulfinch Building
15 New Chardon Street
Boston, Massachusetts 02114
(617) 223-4111

MICHIGAN
Patrick V. McNamara
Federal Building
477 Michigan Avenue
Detroit, Michigan 48226
(313) 226-6280

Genesee Bank Building
352 South Saginaw Street,
Room 200
Flint, Michigan 48502
(313) 234-5109

2922 Fuller Avenue, NE
Grand Rapids, Michigan 49505
(616) 456-2182

MINNESOTA
220 Second Street South
Minneapolis, Minnesota 55401
(612) 349-3000

MISSISSIPPI
Federal Building, Suite 910
100 West Capital Street
Jackson, Mississippi 39269
(601) 960-4738

MISSOURI
Professional Building
1103 Grand Avenue
Kansas City, Missouri 64106
(816) 374-6432

210 North Tucker Blvd.
St. Louis, Missouri 63101
(314) 425-4761

MONTANA
Federal Office Building
301 South Park, Room 340
Helena, Montana 59626
(406) 449-5205

NEBRASKA
Braiker/Brandeis Building
210 South 16th Street
Omaha, Nebraska 68102
(402) 221-3703

NEVADA
1500 E. Tropicana Ave., Suite 205
Las Vegas, Nevada 89119
(702) 388-6500

1050 Bible Way
Post Office Box 4700
Reno, Nevada 89505
(702) 784-5356

NEW HAMPSHIRE
Norris Cotton Federal Building
275 Chestnut Street
Manchester, New Hampshire 03101
(603) 666-7681

NEW JERSEY
Military Park Building
60 Park Place
Newark, New Jersey 07102
(201) 877-1662

The Parkade Building
519 Federal Street
Camden, New Jersey 08103
(609) 757-5081

NEW MEXICO
625 Truman Street, NE
Albuquerque, New Mexico 87110
(505) 262-6463

NEW YORK
26 Federal Plaza
New York, New York 10278
(212) 264-8053

Leo W. O'Brien Federal Building
North Pearl Street & Clinton Ave.
Albany, New York 12207
(518) 472-3567

Mezzanine, Statler Building
107 Delaware Avenue
Buffalo, New York 14202
(716) 846-5755

NORTH CAROLINA
415 North Edgeworth Street
Greensboro, North Carolina 27401
(919) 378-5363

NORTH DAKOTA
Federal Building
Post Office Box 2483
653 2nd Avenue North
Fargo, North Dakota 58102
(701) 239-5136

OHIO
Federal Office Building, Room
9002
550 Main Street
Cincinnati, Ohio 45202
(513) 684-2884

1 Playhouse Square, Rm 420
1375 Euclid Ave.
Cleveland, Ohio 44115
(216) 522-4065

200 North High Street
Clumbus, Ohio 43215
(614) 469-7345

OKLAHOMA
Murrah Federal Building
200 NW 5th Street
Oklahoma City, Oklahoma 73102
(405) 231-4891

Robert S. Kerr Building
440 South Houston Avenue,
Room 200
Tulsa, Oklahoma 74127
(918) 581-7435

OREGON
520 Southwest Sixth Avenue
Portland, Oregon 97204
(503) 221-2561

PENSYLVANIA
Liberty Square Building
105 South Seventh St.
Philadelphia, Pennsylvania 19106
(215) 597-2560

Fort Pitt Commons
412 Old Post Office Courthouse
Pittsburgh, Pennsylvania 15219
(412) 644-6388

PUERTO RICO
159 Carlos Chardon Ave.
San Juan, Puerto Rico 00918
(809) 753-4201

RHODE ISLAND
330 John O. Pastore Federal Bldg.
Providence, Rhode Island 02903
(401) 528-5351

SOUTH CAROLINA
Strom Thurmond Federal Building
1835-45 Assembly Street
Columbia, South Carolina 29201
(803) 765-5592

SOUTH DAKOTA
300 North Dakota Ave., Suite 116
Sioux Falls, South Dakota 57102
(605) 330-4223

TENNESSEE
John J. Duncan Federal Bldg.
710 Locust St., Third Floor
Knoxville, Tennessee 37902
(615) 549-9384

One Memphis Place
200 Jefferson Ave., Suite 1200
Memphis, Tennessee 38103
(901) 521-3367

251 Cumberland Bend Dr., Ste. 200
Nashville, Tennessee 37228
(615) 251-5213

TEXAS
1600 Throckmorton
P.O. Box 2905
Fort Worth, Texas 76113
(817) 885-5401

525 Griffin St., Rm 106
Dallas, Texas 75202
(214) 767-8300

2211 Norfolk Tower, Suite 200
Houston, Texas 77098
(713) 953-3274

Federal Office Building
1205 Texas Avenue
Lubbock, Texas 79401
(806) 743-7265

Washington Square
800 Dolorosa
Post Office Box 9163
San Antonio, Texas 78285
(512) 229-6806

UTAH
324 South State St., Suite 220
Salt Lake City, Utah 84111
(801) 524-5237

VERMONT
Federal Bulding
11 Elmwood Ave., Rm B-311
P.O. Box 1104
Burlington, Vermont 05402
(802) 951-6290

VIRGINIA
701 East Franklin Street
Richmond, Virginia 23219
(804) 771-2721

WASHINGTON
Arcade Plaza Buildling
1321 Second Avenue
Seattle, Washington 98101
(206) 442-5414

West 920 Riverside Avenue
Spokane, Washington 99201
(509) 456-4571

WEST VIRGINIA
405 Capitol St., Suite 708
Charleston, West Virginia 25301
(304) 347-7036

WISCONSIN
Henry S. Reuss Fedreal Plaza
310 West Wisconsin Avenue,
Suite 1380
Milwaukee, Wisconsin 53203
(414) 291-3214

WYOMING
4225 Federal Office Building
Post Office Box 580
100 East B Street
Casper, Wyoming 82601
(307) 261-5252

FNMA OFFICES

Home Office
3900 Wisconsin Ave., NW
Washington, DC 20016
(202)752-7000

Southeastern Regional Office
950 East Paces Ferry Rd.
Atlanta, Georgia 30326
(404)365-6000

Midwestern Regional Office
1 South Wacker Dr. Ste. 3100
Chicago, Illinois 60606
(312)368-6200

Southwestern Regional Office
Two Galleria Tower
13455 Noel Rd. Ste. 600
Dallas, Texas 75240
(214)991-7771

Western Regional Office
135 North Los Robles Ave. Ste. 300
Pasadena, California 91101
(818)568-5000

Northeastern Regional Office
510 Walnut St. 16th floor
Philadelphia, Pensylvania 19106
(215)575-1400

FHLMC OFFICES

Home Office
1771 Business Center Dr.
Reston, Virginia 22090
(703)450-3100

Northeast Regional Office
2231 Crystal Dr. Ste. 900
Arlington, Virginia 22202
(703)685-4500

Southeast Regional Office
2839 Paces Ferry Rd. Ste. 700
Atlanta, Georgia 30339
(404)438-3800

North Central Regional Office
333 Wacker Dr. Ste. 3100
Chicago, Illinois 60606
(312)407-7400

Southwest Regional Office
12222 Merit Dr. Ste. 700
Dallas, Texas 75251
(214)702-2000

Western Regional Office
15303 Ventura Blvd. Ste. 500
Sherman Oaks, California 91403
(818)905-0070

AMORTIZATION TABLE

Most real estate loans are repaid to the lender through an amortization plan. An amortized loan is one in which regular equal payments are made so that all the principal and interest will be completely paid by the maturity date.

The amortization table on the next page can be used to find: interest rate, length until maturity, amount of the loan, and amount of each payment. If you know any three of these you can find the fourth from the table. For example, let's determine how much you must pay each month to amortize a $70,000 loan over 30 years at 11 percent interest. On the amortization table locate the 30 year column. Move down this column until you intersect the row for 11 percent interest; the value the table gives is $9.53. For every $1,000 borrowed you must repay $9.53 per month. In this case your loan was for $70,000, so multiply $9.53 by 70 to get $667.10, which is your monthly payment.

Suppose the interest rate was 12.5%, the length of the loan was for 15 years, and the amount borrowed was $90,000. From the table we can see that the monthly payment per $1000 is $12.33. Multiply this by 90 and you get a total monthly amount of $1109.70.

Amortization tables are most often used to find the payments needed to repay a loan as shown in these examples. But they can also be used to find the size of a loan given a certain monthly payment, number of years until the loan is fully repaid, or the interest rate.

If you can only afford $600 a month and you want to buy a house with a 30-year loan at 12% interest you can figure the maximum amount you can borrow. The table shows $10.29 per $1000 loaned. Dividing $600 by $10.29 gives you 58.309, multiply this by $1000 to get $58,309. This is how much your loan must be to keep monthly payments at $600. It should be noted that this does not take into account taxes and hazard insurance which may also be paid with the monthly mortgage payment.

MONTHLY PAYMENT PER $1000 OF LOAN

Interest Rate per Year	Life of the Loan							
	5 years	10 years	15 years	20 years	25 years	30 years	35 years	40 years
5.0%	$18.88	$10.61	$7.91	$6.60	$5.85	$5.37	$5.05	$4.83
5.5	19.11	10.86	8.18	6.88	6.15	5.68	5.38	5.16
6.0	19.34	11.11	8.44	7.17	6.45	6.00	5.71	5.51
6.5	19.57	11.36	8.72	7.46	6.76	6.32	6.05	5.86
7.0	19.81	11.62	8.99	7.76	7.07	6.66	6.39	6.22
7.5	20.04	11.88	9.28	8.06	7.39	7.00	6.75	6.59
8.0	20.28	12.14	9.56	8.37	7.72	7.34	7.11	6.96
8.5	20.52	12.40	9.85	8.68	8.06	7.69	7.47	7.34
9.0	20.76	12.67	10.15	9.00	8.40	8.05	7.84	7.72
9.5	21.01	12.94	10.45	9.33	8.74	8.41	8.22	8.11
10.0	21.25	13.22	10.75	9.66	9.09	8.78	8.60	8.50
10.5	21.50	13.50	11.06	9.99	9.45	9.15	8.99	8.89
11.0	21.75	13.78	11.37	10.33	9.81	9.53	9.37	9.29
11.5	22.00	14.06	11.69	10.67	10.17	9.91	9.77	9.69
12.0	22.25	14.35	12.01	11.02	10.54	10.29	10.16	10.09
12.5	22.50	14.64	12.33	11.37	10.91	10.68	10.56	10.49
13.0	22.76	14.94	12.66	11.72	11.28	11.07	10.96	10.90
13.5	23.01	15.23	12.99	12.08	11.66	11.46	11.36	11.31
14.0	23.27	15.53	13.32	12.44	12.04	11.85	11.76	11.72
14.5	23.53	15.83	13.66	12.80	12.43	12.25	12.17	12.13
15.0	23.79	16.14	14.00	13.17	12.81	12.65	12.57	12.54
15.5	24.06	16.45	14.34	13.54	13.20	13.05	12.98	12.95
16.0	24.32	16.76	14.69	13.92	13.59	13.45	13.39	13.36
16.5	24.59	17.07	15.04	14.29	13.99	13.85	13.80	13.77
17.0	24.86	17.38	15.39	14.67	14.38	14.26	14.21	14.19
17.5	25.13	17.70	15.75	15.05	14.78	14.67	14.62	14.60
18.0	25.40	18.02	16.11	15.44	15.18	15.08	15.03	15.02
18.5	25.67	18.35	16.47	15.82	15.58	15.48	15.45	15.43
19.0	25.95	18.67	16.83	16.21	15.98	15.89	15.86	15.85
19.5	26.22	19.00	17.20	16.60	16.38	16.30	16.27	16.26
20.0	26.50	19.33	17.57	16.99	16.79	16.72	16.69	16.68
20.5	26.78	19.66	17.94	17.39	17.19	17.13	17.10	17.09
21.0	27.06	20.00	18.31	17.78	17.60	17.54	17.52	17.51
21.5	27.34	20.34	18.69	18.18	18.01	17.95	17.93	17.92
22.0	27.62	20.67	19.06	18.57	18.42	18.36	18.35	18.34
22.5	27.91	21.02	19.44	18.97	18.83	18.78	18.76	18.75
23.0	28.20	21.36	19.82	19.37	19.24	19.19	19.18	19.17
23.5	28.48	21.70	20.20	19.78	19.65	19.61	19.59	19.59
24.0	28.77	22.05	20.59	20.18	20.06	20.02	20.01	20.01
24.5	29.06	22.40	20.97	20.58	20.47	20.43	20.42	20.42
25.0	29.36	22.75	21.36	20.99	20.88	20.85	20.84	20.84

INDEX